Second impression 1977
First published 1976 by
The Hamlyn Publishing Group Limited
London . New York . Sydney . Toronto
Astronaut House, Feltham, Middlesex, England
© Copyright The Hamlyn Publishing Group Limited 1976
ISBN 0 600 33991 2
Printed in Spain by Mateu-Cromo, S.A.

Fishing

with David Carl Forbes

Hamlyn
London . New York . Sydney . Toronto

Dedication

To the many angling friends with whom
I have fished over the years, and in
particular Ted Andrews, Donald Downs,
John Goddard, Joe Perrin, Jack Perry,
and Nigel Widowson.

Special Acknowledgement

Maureen Carl Forbes and the publishers wish to
express their gratitude to the two people who
made it possible to complete this book upon the
sudden death of the author. Donald Downs and
Ted Wade each generously gave their time
and distinctive talents in finishing the captions
and illustrations to the same high standard
of David Carl Forbes.

Contents

Introduction

Man has always fished. Some groups were better than others, leaving the hunting on the plains and making their encampments beside rivers and estuaries, their whole way of life geared to the pursuit of the creatures in freshwater and the sea. When man went in fear of the great animals of the plain, the first fish hook was almost certainly a length of bone, sharpened at both ends and with a place for the line knot notched in the middle. The baited 'hook' would be left out in the water until such time as it was taken by a fish and the bone wedged in its throat. This was not sport but the necessity for survival, the finding of comparatively easy meat when any other was obtained only with the risk of fighting tusked beasts.

By the time that the basic hook shape had evolved, man was not so dependent upon fish as an easy food for survival, but still fish featured strongly in his diet, and still he sought it with hook and line. We cannot tell when necessity gave way to sport, but in the angling books of the 1700s, anglers

Right: in the 1700s, and early 1800s, spikes with revolving tops to carry the line and tackle were often staked out overnight to catch fish.

8

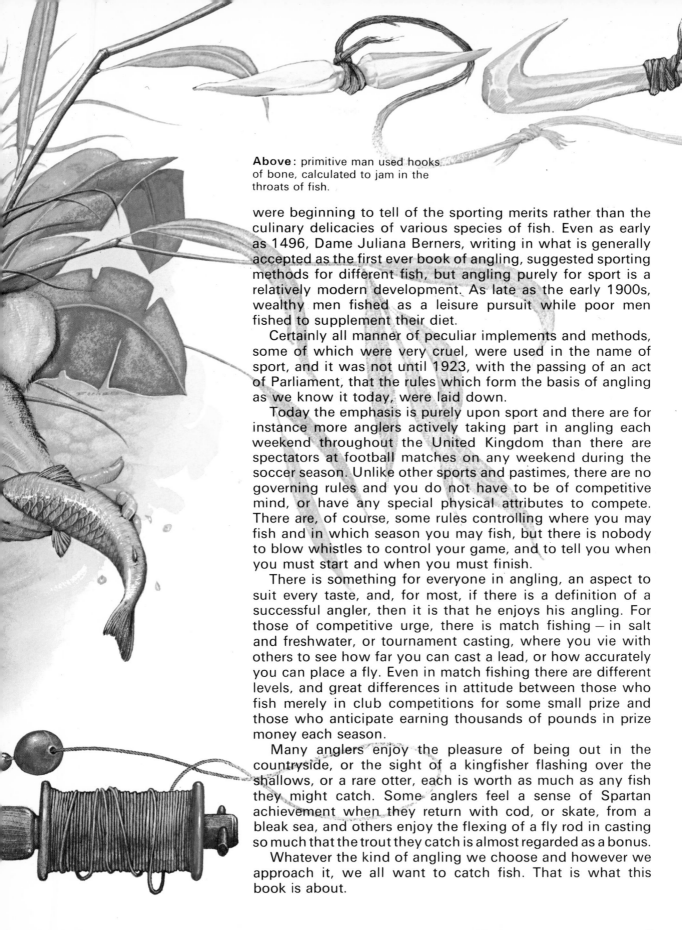

Above: primitive man used hooks of bone, calculated to jam in the throats of fish.

were beginning to tell of the sporting merits rather than the culinary delicacies of various species of fish. Even as early as 1496, Dame Juliana Berners, writing in what is generally accepted as the first ever book of angling, suggested sporting methods for different fish, but angling purely for sport is a relatively modern development. As late as the early 1900s, wealthy men fished as a leisure pursuit while poor men fished to supplement their diet.

Certainly all manner of peculiar implements and methods, some of which were very cruel, were used in the name of sport, and it was not until 1923, with the passing of an act of Parliament, that the rules which form the basis of angling as we know it today, were laid down.

Today the emphasis is purely upon sport and there are for instance more anglers actively taking part in angling each weekend throughout the United Kingdom than there are spectators at football matches on any weekend during the soccer season. Unlike other sports and pastimes, there are no governing rules and you do not have to be of competitive mind, or have any special physical attributes to compete. There are, of course, some rules controlling where you may fish and in which season you may fish, but there is nobody to blow whistles to control your game, and to tell you when you must start and when you must finish.

There is something for everyone in angling, an aspect to suit every taste, and, for most, if there is a definition of a successful angler, then it is that he enjoys his angling. For those of competitive urge, there is match fishing – in salt and freshwater, or tournament casting, where you vie with others to see how far you can cast a lead, or how accurately you can place a fly. Even in match fishing there are different levels, and great differences in attitude between those who fish merely in club competitions for some small prize and those who anticipate earning thousands of pounds in prize money each season.

Many anglers enjoy the pleasure of being out in the countryside, or the sight of a kingfisher flashing over the shallows, or a rare otter, each is worth as much as any fish they might catch. Some anglers feel a sense of Spartan achievement when they return with cod, or skate, from a bleak sea, and others enjoy the flexing of a fly rod in casting so much that the trout they catch is almost regarded as a bonus.

Whatever the kind of angling we choose and however we approach it, we all want to catch fish. That is what this book is about.

Coarse Fishing

Generally, all the fish to be caught in freshwater, with the exception of trout and salmon, are known as *coarse* fish. The origin of the term coarse, used to group the various species of fish caught in ponds, lakes, streams and rivers, is obscure and indeed strange, for there is nothing coarse about the stream-lined shape of a barbel or the sleek flank of a dace. And certainly the tackle of the so-called coarse fisherman can be as fine as any you will see employed in any aspect of angling.

Coarse fish are found in abundance right throughout Europe in all kinds of waters, and wherever you live, you will find fishing for several species — even if you live in the heart of London or Paris.

What you can learn about the fish you are seeking, and the nature of the water in which they live, is much more important than owning a great range of expensive fishing tackle, but obviously we must have some form of tackle. We shall start by considering the very basics.

The absolute essentials for catching fish are hook and line. Using a bait which a fish will accept as natural food, you *could* creep cautiously to the water, lower your tackle into place, and catch fish quite easily — but it will not work all the time. In order to be able to put your bait and hook further out, you need a rod and, to hold the line and make casting easy, a reel. These are the essentials and, while it is nice to own all those attractive baubles that make up the fishing tackle collection, you really do not need anything else for many fishing situations.

To know for certain that a fish has taken your bait, to keep your bait up in the water, and to help your bait to travel along the current in a river, you will need floats. To make the weight for long distance casting and to keep the bait where you want it in the water, you will need leads.

These are refinements to help you use the essentials of tackle to best advantage, and while there are many other aids to make angling easier, you may still catch fish without them.

Unfortunately, there is no such thing as an all-purpose fishing-rod, but there are many tubular glass fibre rods available and suitable for general fishing. No reputable fishing tackle dealer will recommend those short, plastic 'pokers' commonly called 'boys' rods', for most dealers are anglers themselves and appreciate that a rod needs to be at least 10 feet long (300 cm*). On choosing a rod, you must ensure that the dealer understands that you require a 'general' course fishing rod for such fish as roach and bream, and not a powerful, specialist rod such as that needed for pike or big carp. That type of rod, if you decide to try for big fish, can come later when you understand the basics of angling.

Above: one of the better type of fixed-spool reel on the market, this one incorporates all the sound technical principles for simple and efficient use. For more information see page 38.

* *All metric measurement equivalents are approximate.*

You will need a fixed-spool reel and although these come in all price ranges the most *in*expensive is quite adequate for your needs at this stage. As this is the general purpose reel in angling it is discussed at length on page 38. Also, while you are learning to fish, a monofilament line of five pounds (2·5 kg) breaking strain is ideal. Most dealers (if not approached at a very busy time!) will load your reel with line for you.

Hooks are inexpensive and available in many sizes, but the numbers used to identify hook sizes may cause some confusion at the beginning. What you have to remember is that the smaller the hook so the larger the number identifying it. For our purposes, the smallest hook you will need (for roach, rudd, dace and gudgeon) is a number 16, while the largest (for barbel, bream, chub and tench) will be a number eight. Eventually, you may wish to try for carp or pike, and then you will have to think about the very big hooks such as a 4 or a 2.

To start, buy your small hooks — numbers 16, 14, and 12 — in what is known as 'to nylon'. These hooks come in small envelopes, and each hook is attached to a length of fine nylon, finished with a loop which joins the main line on your reel. The larger hooks — numbers 10 and 8 — are usually for larger fish, and these hooks are generally available as 'loose'

Above: a satisfying mixed bag for a morning's freelining in a small stream — one pike, two perch and some chub.

Below: this plump roach in prime condition fell to a trotted maggot.

11

Right: compartmented shot containers are nice to own, but they may offer some sizes of shot you will seldom use and the *container* may cost *more* than the shot it holds. Most fishing tackle dealers stock small polythene tubs containing shot of specific sizes, and this is the most inexpensive way of buying lead weights.

Dust shot

Swan shot

Drilled bullets

Hooks-to-nylon

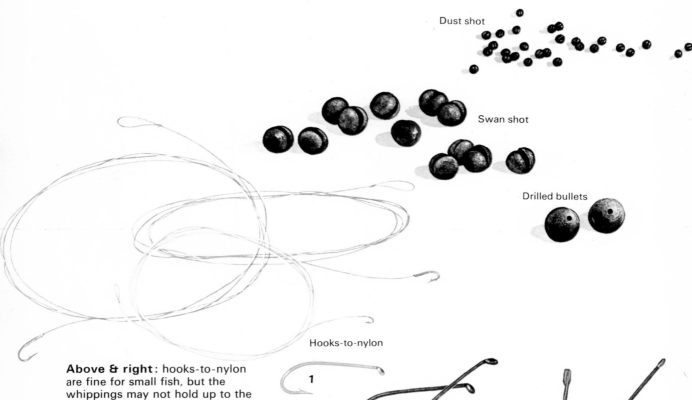

Above & right: hooks-to-nylon are fine for small fish, but the whippings may not hold up to the power of a big fish. Although there is not much to choose between hooks at this stage, though they should be sharp and well-tempered, these are some you will see in tackle shops:
1 — Gilt
2 — Blued
3 — Bronzed Long Shank
4 — Bronzed Short Shank
5 — Spade-end
6 — Straight-eye

or 'plain' hooks, that is, not attached to lengths of nylon, but with an eye at the top to enable you to connect your hook direct to the main reel line.

Look at the knots on page 57 and you will see the simple whipping used to connect large hooks to the line. *Regard every knot in your line as a weak point, and consider the strongest outfit you can have has merely one knot connecting your hook to the main line.* Fine, looped hook lengths are all right for small fish such as roach and dace, but you need strong tackle throughout for fish such as barbel or bream, which may weigh several pounds or kilograms.

Floats are designed to react according to conditions, depending upon whether you are fishing in rivers or ponds, and in some cases to enable you to float-fish even in very strong winds, and so you will encounter a great range of all shapes and sizes. In this case, you will have to tell the tackle dealer the sort of water you are likely to fish, what sort of fish you expect to catch, and rely purely upon his advice. Basically, you will need slender floats for still waters and more substantial, 'trotting' floats for rivers and streams.

In order to balance your float in the water, and also as an aid to casting, you need weight on the line in the form of split-shot. Available in various sizes, the smallest shot is termed dust-shot, the largest, swan-shot. Split-shot is

Right: the majority of these floats are home-made and are designed to carry small or large amounts of weight — they are painted in colours that will enable them to be seen under varying light conditions. Making your own float can be great fun and very rewarding: elder pith, cork and balsa wood are ideal for making buoyant bodies and sanded splits of bamboo make good antenna. Feather quills when cleaned and painted also make excellent slender floats.

generally sold in containers with a specific size of shot or offering a selection of the various sizes. Start off with a compartmented box of mixed shot which will enable you to choose the right size of shot to suit any situation.

The best float-makers indicate the size and amount of shot necessary to balance a particular float correctly in the water, but when this information is not available it is best, as a general guide to add shot to the line until merely half an inch (1·5 cm) of the float tip shows above water. A well-cocked float can be cast easily and offers least resistance to a taking fish, and the modern paints in use allow even a small tip of colour to be seen from long distances.

Floats seem to fascinate anglers and few, whatever their age, can resist building up a large collection. If you consider that different floats will be needed to deal with clear or murky water, with slow glides of current and relative torrents, for fishing close-in and at long range, or for remaining in position even though a gale is blowing across a lake, you will appreciate that you need different floats for different situations.

It is not possible to tell you what float to use, because I cannot appreciate the conditions of the water on the day you are to fish it. Your choice will rest on common sense and a thoughtful approach — which is what makes the difference between the successful and the average angler.

Moving away from the actual basics of tackle, a landing net is a very important item. You cannot lift out a fish of any appreciable size on the strength of the rod alone. If you acquire a large net you could avoid losing an unexpectedly large fish at the final moment. The run-of-the-mill fish may look fairly silly in a large landing net, but a large net is justified if it enables you to beat just one great fish which you may never forget.

If you want to retain your catch until the end of the day — and most of us do — then, you need a keep-net and, again, it should be the largest you can afford. Scales and fins become damaged when lots of small fish, or one large one, are cramped in a small net. For humane reasons, and future sport, you should return your fish unharmed at the end of the day.

The equipment we have considered up to now will give you a good chance of catching fish under many conditions, and you will catch more fish by fully understanding the tackle you have and the water you are to fish, than you will by learning a great mass of complicated tackles and techniques. At this stage, you will be a relatively complete angler if you add **legering** to your repertoire.

When legering, we do not use floats but merely a lead, which either has a channel through which the line passes or an 'eye' attachment. There are various designs of leads, and generally they are used either to enable us to cast long distances out into deep water, or to keep the bait — either stationary or rolling — down on the bottom in a fast current.

To know that a fish has taken the bait, we have to have some form of bite indicator on the rod itself, or in rare cases, to rely upon the tip of the rod moving.

Legering enables us to fish very deep water which could not be conveniently fished with float tackle and also, when necessary, to keep a bait in an area where float tackle would be washed away by fast water. You may either hold the rod and watch for or feel bites vibrate on the tip — which is a very good way to catch fish in fast rivers, or lay the rod on two rests and rely upon some form of indicator showing the bites — which is the standard method on lakes and ponds. Casting with this tackle is very simple, but for technique when using a fixed-spool reel see page 38.

With the tackle and the two main forms of coarse fishing, float and leger, I have already mentioned, we could go out and catch all manner of fish efficiently, but still there are

Landing net

Keep net

Opposite & below: be considerate to the fish. Get the largest landing net and keep net that you can afford. A good pair of artery forceps will remove the hook cleanly and prevent permanent damage. Two rod rests enable the rod position to be adjusted to suit conditions. Several bait boxes will be necessary if a number of different baits are required.

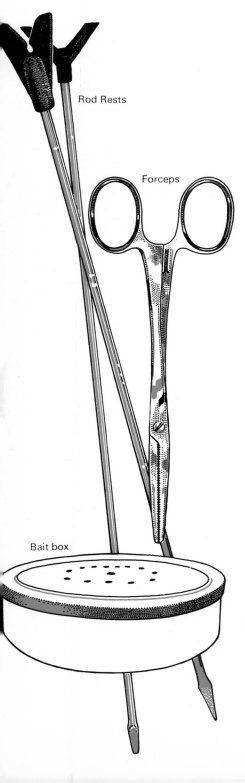

Rod Rests

Forceps

Bait box

many refinements and accessories which add to the ease and comfort of angling. Forceps for removing hooks, rod rests, some form of seating, and bait boxes, are some which come readily to mind.

Before we consider the characteristics of the fish we are after, I want you to appreciate that we are setting out to catch wild creatures which lack the brain capacity of man, but in lacking our intelligence they more than compensate by the manner in which they respond to our presence close to their environment. Unlike us, fish have nothing in their life to distract them from the essentials of feeding and surviving, and their life is constantly attuned to danger. How close do you think you could walk to a wild deer or rabbit in a field? Well, fish are exactly the same, but because they live in a different element, you cannot always see how they react to our presence. Those fish may not see us approach the river or lake, but they will almost certainly know we have arrived because of the noise we make, which is transmitted to them by vibrations through the soil and water.

It is a fact that many anglers do not miss fish through faulty fishing, but simply because they have scared away the fish they are attempting to catch.

No matter how inexperienced you are — and not all expert anglers are elderly — you can catch the biggest fish in the water if you can put a bait to that fish without it knowing you are there. It should be obvious that you cannot catch fish where there are none to be caught, but walk along a river bank, or watch some of your friends next time out, and you will see anglers scaring fish away before they begin fishing. When sedge and other foliage is beaten down to make a nice pitch, the activity sends the fish rocketing away, and when you hammer rod rests into the bank, the ensuing vibrations also frighten fish. Would you expect fish to remain in your vicinity when you reach out to break off a dead branch that might spoil casting, or if you walked to the edge in your new white shirt and waved to friends on the other bank?

You often hear people say that you must not talk when you go fishing, but talking does not matter, for such sound seldom penetrates the surface of the water. What you must not do, is to place yourself fully in view of the fish, or cause disturbances which may reach the fish. When you prepare for exams in biology, you will find that fish possess a sense unknown to any form of land animal. This sense is indicated in a line along the fish's flank, known as the lateral line, and it picks up vibrations and pressure changes in water. You can see how easily your shadow on the water scares fish, but you may not appreciate that they have gone because of your heavy tread, or because you hammered a rod rest into a hard bank.

Learn to move around the water with caution, using whatever natural cover the bank offers, and you may catch a lot of fish long before you have learned to cast well or have amassed a fund of angling information. No matter how technically fine an angler you are, you still find that the really big fish fall to the right bait placed with stealth and caution.

If you bear this all in mind, you will find that catching fish is really a very easy pastime, and becomes complicated only when you decide that you are going to catch fish of a certain species, or of a particular size. Initially, of course, you will want merely to catch a fish of any kind, and then you will want to catch as many of those fish as you can, and eventually try to catch as many different kinds of fish as you can. In the course of doing this, your casting and fishing technique will be improving, and when the next stage arrives — the desire to catch a very big fish of a particular species, you will be sufficiently experienced to cope with it. Angling is a wonderful pastime in that you do not have to be strong or athletic to excel in it, and you do not have to study it for years before you become successful at it.

The **baits** which anglers use are legion, some coming from natural sources and others requiring quite elaborate preparation. The most easily acquired of all these baits is the earthworm, and in my fishing it rates as the supreme all-round bait. Brandlings and small redworms may be collected from

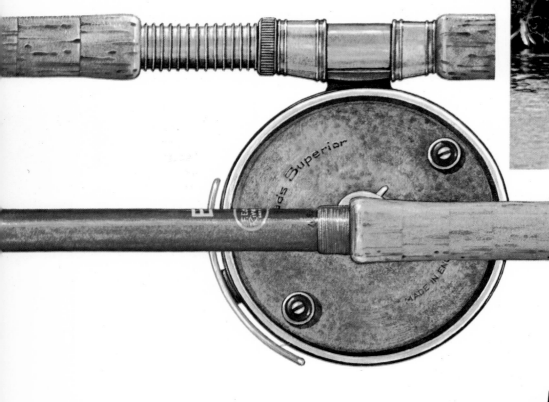

Above: reel fittings are normally either screw-type — fixed in one place, or sliding rings — which enable you to place the reel on the handle where you wish. While the traditional, round, centre-pin reel is still available — mainly for piking — it is out-dated by the fixed-spool reel for general coarse fishing.

Opposite above: when ready to net a big fish, try to contain your excitement and pause to see what the fish is doing. Then lower the landing net and pull your fish over it. Never chase the fish with the net. In this joint venture, the young angler stops retrieving line to wait for the net to submerge.

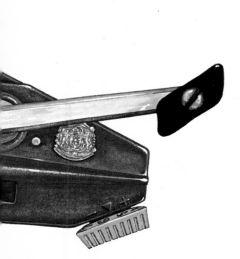

compost heaps and beneath stones or logs, while huge lobworms may be dug from clay soil, or gathered from the lawn at night with the aid of a torch. There is no fish in freshwater, whether it is the tiny gudgeon or the majestic salmon, that will not take a worm at some time or another.

Maggots, or gentles, are the common bait of the coarse fish angler. They can be purchased readily from tackle shops and they require no preparation. They are convenient bait and, considering that we will be embarking on a course of catching a fish of any kind or amassing a netful of small fish, maggots are almost essential.

The third bait we shall consider is bread. We need no other baits, for we can — by choosing carefully from a small selection and fishing with care — equal anything that may be caught by other anglers who chose to make an unnecessary science of the matter. To make our bread into paste, it is best to have an unsliced loaf which is at least one day old. To use the bread as what is known as *flake*, we need the freshest loaf obtainable and sliced bread is ideal for this purpose. There is no preparation in advance, we merely take the loaf to the bank-side with us.

For paste, I tear the crumb out of the stale loaf and dip it

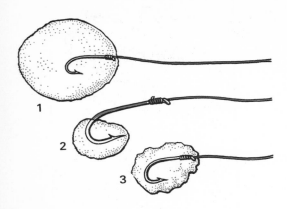

Above: fig 1 shows the bait muffling the point of the hook thus spoiling the effect of the strike, while fig 2 shows the opposite — too little on just the bend and the point. Fig 3 shows the ideal, the hook covered completely but not muffling the point.

quickly into the water so that I can get it wet enough to knead. Once I can work it between my fingers, I keep dipping it quickly into the water and kneading until the paste has absorbed sufficient water to be of the right consistency. Unfortunately, this is one of those things that cannot be described and good bread paste comes about through experience. What you have to consider, is that you must not have a paste so stiff that it forms a hard pellet about the hook — otherwise, when a fish bites, it may merely pull the pellet of bread out without the hook penetrating. Ideally, bread paste should only just stay on the hook, and if you keep withdrawing the tackle with the paste intact, it is almost certainly too stiff. You have to cover the hook completely, and a bait which muffles the point of the hook when you strike is, of course, worthless. You will hook fish easily with soft bread-paste, but expect the mild inconvenience of having to re-bait for each cast.

With a combination of hook bait and carefully laid ground-bait, there is no reason at all why we should not catch a lot of fish on the first trip out. In a lake, we throw a handful of maggots out into an area of relatively deep water within range of casting ability, and then make up the tackle with a small hook carrying two maggots. We fish in that area, occasionally throwing in a few more maggots and gradually pushing the float up the line until we are fishing at a depth that gives fish. If there are rudd present, we will catch them high in the water, and a few small roach also, but as the bait gets close to the bottom, we would expect to start catching larger roach, the occasional tench, bream, or perhaps a succession of perch.

In a river, a handful of maggots can be sent down on the current at regular intervals to concentrate the fish into an area which, to them appears as a food lane. Then maggots on a hook are sent along the current, carried beneath a float which is allowed to travel at the speed of the current without any check in movement. Again, the float is pushed up the line until the effective depth to catch fish is found. The float is allowed to run down on the current for a distance of 20 or 25 yards (20 or 25 m), retrieved, and then sent down again. This is **long-trotting.**

You could expect to catch dace anywhere along the maggot trail, and gudgeon, roach, bream, perch, or even barbel, when the float gets into the area where the maggots are settling. Keep a direct line on the surface between rod tip and float, without checking the movement of the float and after the first fish, be prepared to strike as the float goes back into the area in which it was hooked.

Most of the time, the success of the venture depends upon the amount of bait you put in for ground bait and the intervals at which it is introduced. Obviously, you will not want to create a mound of food in still water, or your hook bait will have no attraction. On the other hand, you should not put in such a small amount that it is insufficient to hold the interest of the fish in the area you are fishing.

In running water, you have to gauge the flow in order to

Below: shotting is important — if placed too near to the hook the shot can pull the bait quickly down past the level at which the fish may be feeding. Shot placed more closely to the float will enable the bait to sink at its own speed and give the fish a greater chance to find it on the way down.

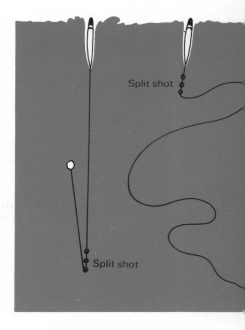

keep the fish feeding in an area where you can reach them. If you put handfuls of maggots in too frequently — particularly in very fast water, the fish may go chasing off downstream after maggots and get beyond the range in which you can control your float tackle. If you do not put in enough maggots, the shoal may work upstream looking for more until they are almost under your rod tip and the first movement you make frightens them away.

This is where the thoughtful approach, and some trial and error, may earn you a lot of fish.

Once you have started the shoals of small fish feeding, big fish of various species may be attracted into the area by the activity. If you have been catching small roach or dace on almost every trot, and suddenly a bite results in a fish that seems unstoppable, or you bring a big fish to your net after a seemingly frightening struggle, you will have to revise your tackle.

That tiny hook-to-nylon may have been all right for small fish, but it could cost you big specimens as you try to haul them upstream against the current. Feed in another handful of maggots to keep the fish interested, and then remove that small hook-to-nylon. Now you should whip on an eyed hook direct to the main reel line, and the size of that hook will depend upon the species of fish in the swim. If they are big roach, then a number 12 hook is as large as you need to go, and, as you have already caught one on maggots, it is safe to assume you will catch more. You connect the hook, bait with maggots and carry on the procedure.

If your one big fish is a chub, or a perch, then whip on a big, number 8 hook and, although keeping the maggots going down on the current, change your hook bait to a large worm. Where perch are concerned, you may take one after another, for perch are shoal fish and an encounter with a shoal could result in the catch of a lifetime. It *could* be exactly the same with chub, but there is a chance that merely one big fish moved into the small fry.

If your big hook and worm results in lots of bites but no fish, then you will have to chance that the big one you have taken was a solitary specimen, and the small roach and dace are still active. Take off the big hook and re-connect with the small hook-to-nylon with maggot bait.

It may seem to be a chore, this changing of hooks and baits, when fish are obviously active, but you must consider that, in return for your laziness in not bothering to increase the strength of your tackle, you could well have your fine hook length broken by a very big fish.

I know because it has happened to me on both counts. I have carried on fishing with fine tackle because I could not be bothered to change — and gone home with tales of fish breaking away. I have also changed tackle time after time without success when other anglers were taking dozens of small fish — but in the last hour had a succession of big fish which made those other anglers gasp.

If you work on a routine of using **ground-bait** carefully

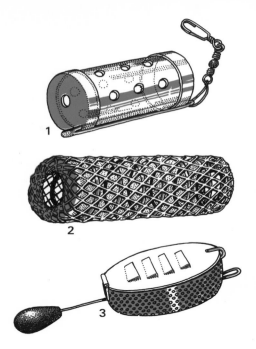

Above: fig 1 shows a swimfeeder which is a perforated plastic tube that has been weighted with a strip of lead and has a swivel attached at one end so that the line can be run through and stopped, to enable it to be used as a leger weight. Maggots or other bait are put into the tube and the ends plugged with bread or clay. The swimfeeder is then cast into the water and the maggots escape through the perforations providing a steady stream of ground bait, close to the baited hook. The hair roller shown at fig 2 can be used as a substitute. Fig 3 shows a bait dropper which places ground bait accurately in running water. It consists of a container which has a hinged lid which is secured by a wire with a lead weight at one end. The container is filled with maggots and the hook passed through the eye on the right hand side and then set in a pad of cork at the back. The dropper is then lowered into the swim. The lead reaches the bottom first and the jolt springs the catch, opening the lid and releasing the maggots. The line is then reeled in, the dropper removed and the hook baited for fishing.

to attract fish into your fishing area, whether in still or moving water, you should have no difficulty in catching fish of some sort; although generally these will be small. The important thing is to ply your tackle accurately in the area you have ground-baited. Normally, this is easiest in moving water, for then the ground bait is running along a route dictated by the current and your float will follow this route; finding fish moving up the ground bait trail or eventually passing over the spot where the ground bait is settling.

It is not so easy in lakes and ponds, and the larger the water and the greater the range of your casting, so the more difficult it becomes. Bear in mind that it is virtually impossible to throw ground bait into a featureless expanse of water and to know exactly where it has fallen when you come to cast. If you do not use some imaginary form of markers — such as trees or other high points on the skyline — to indicate

Left: a young angler proudly displays a fine grayling taken on a trotted maggot.

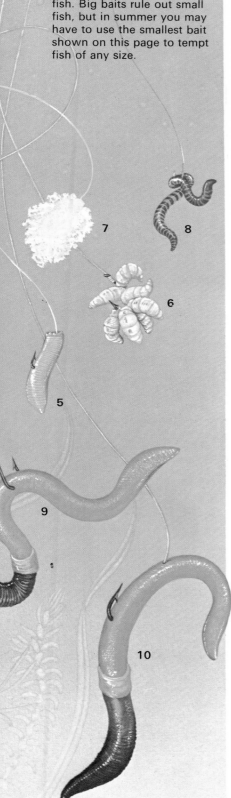

Right: anglers always argue over baits and hooks, but 5, 7, 9 and 10, are the types and sizes I normally use. This helps me to catch fish of the size shown here, and I am happy with fewer but bigger fish. Big baits rule out small fish, but in summer you may have to use the smallest bait shown on this page to tempt fish of any size.

7

8

6

5

9

10

exactly where your ground bait has gone in, you may cast again and again and never put your hook into the right area.

Experienced anglers have their own ideas about ground-baiting, but I believe in putting small amounts regularly into a small area and getting my hook accurately into that small area. Towards this end, I make a mental note of where imaginary lines from trees, headlands and such objects meet in the water, and this system of cross-reference will enable you to know exactly where to place each fresh portion of ground bait and where to cast your tackle afterwards. When float fishing, I normally cast beyond the area and then retrieve slowly until my float is exactly where I believe my ground bait to be.

When legering, you fish only the bottom regions of the water and have to be really accurate to keep the hook in the ground bait area. With a float, you may pick up small fish at all levels in the water as they rise for slowly sinking particles of ground bait and your hook will sink relatively slowly through these particles. When legering, the tackle plummets straight to the bottom and, if you have not cast accurately your ground bait will have attracted fish to one area while your hook is lying in another.

In really fast rivers you may find float tackle difficult to control because of the rushing water, and on these occasions the **rolling leger** can help you to take fish. Do not use ground bait now, because we shall be rolling the tackle *across* the current instead of letting it run down with the current, and ground bait may take fish away from our fishing area as they follow it downstream.

My drawing shows how the rolling leger is fished. You move along the bank to cover as much water as possible, casting across to the far bank, closing the reel, and letting the current roll the leger back under your own bank, and in this way you are going to fish rather than waiting for them to come to you. You can catch fish of many species with this technique, but I tend to keep it for winter months when there is little weed to snag the progress of my tackle.

You hold the rod all the time now, and bites are seen or felt on the tip. These bites may register as a persistent tremor, a quick jag-jag-jag at the tip, or by the rod pulling right over. Whatever, strike immediately. There will be many false indications as the leger rolls against stones, but after a while you get the feel of knocks from obstructions and let them pass untouched. I make a practice of striking at anything which differs from the normal current movement and, once I have the feel of the current, find that I can tell what is a fish and what is a stone.

Newcomers to angling — of all ages — seem to think that most fish are to be found a great distance out, and on most rivers you see nine out of ten anglers trying to cast right across to the far bank. Now think about it. If they were standing on that far bank, they would be trying to cast their baits right in front of where they are now standing. Of course, sometimes we have to fish far out because, particularly in summer, bank-side disturbance drives the fish far out, but in an ideal angling situation there is no need to cast great distances.

On many rivers and streams — if there is nobody else stamping up and down the bank and you move quietly — you may catch more fish right under the bank than you will in the main current. In fact, most of the biggest fish I have taken have come about through creeping up to the edge of the water and lowering a bait gently (with no float or lead on the line) down through the bank-side foliage. Many of these

Below: make your cast downstream, across to the far bank, and let the current roll it back under your own bank. Continue downstream in this manner. (Insert) a split shot stops the drilled bullet from falling down over the hook. Lacking a bullet, you can improvise with several split-shot nipped onto nylon which has been looped over the main line.

Current

22

fish came from tiny streams no more than fifteen feet (450 cm) wide, which looked incapable of holding good fish and consequently were neglected by other anglers.

This sort of fishing can be productive and very exciting, and often bears no relationship to the normal fishing scene, where you sit on a basket and fish a broad expanse of water with float or leger. Now you travel lightly with rod and landing net, bait and spare hooks in your pocket, planning to stalk quietly along a length of stream looking for fish. This is a fine way to catch chub, with the most simple rig there is. You merely whip a number 8 hook direct to your five pound (2·5 kg) reel line and rely upon a marble-size ball of bread, or a big worm, to give you the weight for casting.

This is **free-lining,** and often there is no need for casting as such involved. On a hot summer's day, wearing plimsolls or bumpers, you creep through sedge and around bushes like an Apache, looking for dark water under the bank into which you can lower the worm. There is no mistaking when a fish takes, for the line tightens on the water and, if you miss that first indication, the rod tip thumps over. This is the method of the 'specimen-hunter', who wants to catch perhaps just one outstandingly large fish, rather than a net of small fish like every one else catches. Part of the reputations of famous anglers like Richard Walker and Fred J. Taylor have been made by big fish taken on free lines from snaggy, neglected waters. The method is likely to bring you your first big fish, probably a chub, but as likely a perch or wild, brown trout, and you may get them from waters seeming hardly big enough to contain them.

The first angling book was published in 1496, and an uninterrupted flow of angling literature ever since has resulted

Above: this fish fell to rolling leger technique (when I had left my landing net half a mile upstream) and had to be brought out by hand. As when using a landing net, you never chase after the fish, but remain still and bring the fish towards your hand until it is well within reach. Then you bend and grasp the fish firmly by the head. Never stick your fingers into the gill clefts — this kills fish! — and never walk into water to retrieve fish where you cannot see the bottom.

23

Roach

Rudd.

Above: roach and rudd are often confused in identification. The rudd tends to be bronze coloured, but never judge fish by their colour. See how the lower jaw of the roach recedes, while that of the rudd protrudes, and note the top fin of the rudd is set well back.

in angling being surrounded in mystique and masses of complicated techniques. In time, you will enjoy the technicalities yourself, but for now the few methods we have covered here, practised with care and caution, will yield all the fish you want. You can catch more fish than anybody else in your area if you get to know one water really well and practice the method which makes it yield its fish.

You may care to travel from water to water, in which case you may never understand any of them, but if you determine to fish that small pond in your locality or that stream below the hedgerow, with time you will know how best to catch the crucian carp, or where the roach and the chub are most likely to be. Remember, the best anglers do not necessarily have the best tackle and the best technique, but they do understand the waters they fish and know what works best on those waters. A famous angling friend of mine travels miles to fish just one river every winter, and he never uses anything other than float tackle with bread for bait. In the course of just one winter, that man will take more really big roach and chub than the majority of anglers will ever see in a lifetime.

Small fish of all species tend to be found together in large numbers and although different fish have different ways of feeding, this is not noticeable when the fish are merely a few inches or centimetres long. Consequently, you may put ground bait into a lake or pond and attract a great collection of fish to your maggot or worm bait. Once these fish begin a feeding frenzy — which often occurs on early evenings on very hot summer days, you could find even small tench and carp — which normally feed on the bottom, coming up to compete with roach, rudd, and perch. It is only when the fish begin to grow to appreciable size that they form their own shoals and begin to display habits peculiar to themselves.

Bream tend to be greedy feeders, keeping to the lake or river bed and shovelling up the mud in an almost constant search for food. Tench seem to feed in a similar manner,

Below: even experienced anglers confuse these two, but you should have no problems if you look carefully at the shapes of their anal fins — underneath, near the tail. Dace fins are concave, while chub fins are convex. Also, the chub has a much larger mouth.

Chub

Dace

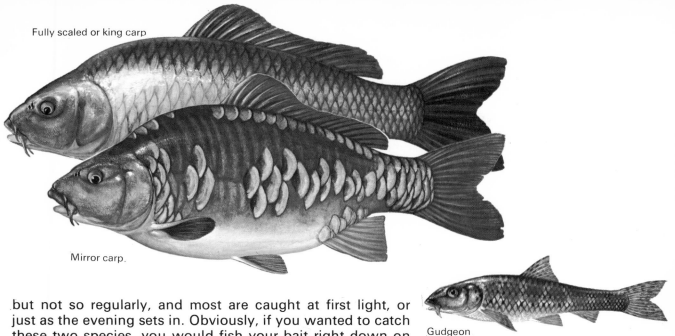

Fully scaled or king carp

Mirror carp.

Gudgeon

but not so regularly, and most are caught at first light, or just as the evening sets in. Obviously, if you wanted to catch these two species, you would fish your bait right down on the bed.

The larger roach tend to feed on the lake bed and keep to the lower regions, but they are disturbed by the mud clouds created by bream and tench and instead choose to search for food over a clean bed, such as gravel. Again, you would fish your bait on the bed, or just above it, and try to fish away from mud banks or soft clay.

Rudd feed mainly in the upper regions and — particularly on hot summer afternoons — right on the surface of the water. Obviously, to catch these fish, there would be no point in throwing out a leger that would plummet down past them. A slowly sinking bait normally accounts for rudd, so you should push your split-shot well up from the hook in order to make the float cock on the surface while your bait is sinking slowly.

Above & below: with the exception of crucian carp and the gudgeon which is tiny, the fish shown here can grow very big and may call for sturdy tackle. The mirror carp is easily distinguished from the king carp by its patches of large scales, but when all are small, the crucian carp can cause confusion. Look at the shape of their top fins, and note that the crucian has no barbels at the mouth.

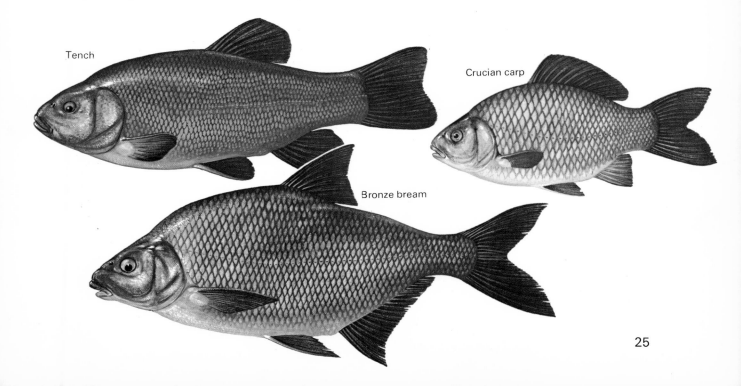

Tench

Crucian carp

Bronze bream

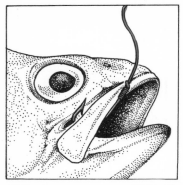

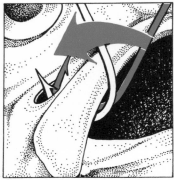

Above & opposite: to remove the hook from a fish effectively, you must first have a firm grip upon it – as well-known British angler, Fred J. Taylor, shows opposite. You can use fingers for big hooks, but forceps are surer for small hooks. When a fish is hooked in the nerveless membrane around the mouth, as shown in the diagrams above, just move the hook to disengage the barb and slip it down, and out. If the hook has been swallowed, never probe, but merely cut the nylon close to the fish's mouth – fish have their own way of disposing of hooks! Hooks come out easily if you remember that you have to clear the barb from its hold before attempting to withdraw.

Chub like to shelter in tree roots and all manner of obstructions in the water, as do perch, and so the angler seeking these two species searches out the areas around tree stumps and lily-beds; often with a free-line and worm bait, cast to sink slowly with attractive wriggles and twists.

Dace are shoal fish, most commonly found where shallow water runs quickly over gravel, and where you have caught one, you may well catch another dozen. They have small mouths – unlike perch and chub, which can engulf almost any bait – and so you have to use small hooks and small baits which they can snatch quickly in the fast water.

I believe that most success in angling comes from understanding the quarry, and to catch fish consistently – not just now and again, by pure luck – you have to know what they feed upon, how they feed, and the areas in which they are most likely to find their food. Knowing this, you employ a bait which looks or moves like it should be eaten, and fish it in an area where fish would expect to find it.

Now, fish are not distributed throughout water like currants in a cake. They are concentrated in certain areas because there is an attraction in that area, and most of the time that attraction is food. Once you begin to understand this, you start to fish where the fish are, rather than waste time fishing 'empty' water.

For example, perch feed upon insects and small fish. These small fry are to be found in the vicinity of weed clumps, so the perch hides in the weeds. As it grows larger, it needs larger prey, and now it spends some time in ambush among lily stalks, sedge clumps, and tree roots, where the dark bands on its flanks provide camouflage in keeping with the surroundings.

Chub are often found in fast rivers, but they do not like to spend their time battling incessantly against the current to avoid being swept downstream. Instead, they lurk in gaps in the bank and behind boulders, enjoying the ease of the sheltered water and waiting to dash out to feed upon whatever the current brings close to them. This is why the free-lined bait, fished close-in, is often so very effective.

Bream do not like to fight against the current either, which is why you will often find them in the lee of big bends in the river, where the current deflects and leaves slow, deep pools, with accumulations of silt in which the fish browse.

These are fairly typical examples, but I cannot say for certain where you may expect to find certain fish, for no two rivers or lakes are alike and much will depend upon the nature of the current or the contours of a lake bed. And, of course, what holds good on a particular river on one day may change the next with an increase in current due to heavy rainfall, or lock gates being opened upstream. This is why it is important to get to know a particular water as well as you can, for gradually a pattern emerges and you begin to know where to find fish under certain conditions.

A river has two faces: a gentle, clear flow in summer and a raging flood of coloured water in winter. If you understand the river and what makes the fish keep to certain parts of it, you will be able to catch fish no matter what the time of year.

Consider that floods scour out the river at its middle and no form of food will stay there in winter. Neither will the fish want to fight against the darkly-coloured torrent. Food will settle in the small slacks close to the bank, and it is in these places that the fish are feeding and recovering from the confusion of the flood. I have taken dozens of fish of all species and sizes on many occasions from tiny slacks on the edge of fast water. At this time of year, with heavy rain, all manner of normally dormant insects and worms are being washed from the soil. Is it really surprising that my biggest fish have fallen to lobworms swirling slowly on the verge of a flood?

Carp and Pike Fishing

Because **carp** and **pike** are the leviathans of the freshwater world, and therefore require more powerful tackle to fish than the species already discussed, we shall treat them separately. However before studying the tackle and techniques you should know something about them.

The British record carp — taken in 1953 by Richard Walker, weighed 44 pounds (22 kg). On several occasions, pike in excess of 50 pounds have been recorded in the British Isles. All anglers like to daydream about huge fish, but most experienced anglers appreciate that such giant fish are the rareties of angling, encountered only by the few and but once in a lifetime.

Now, by the standards just reported, a 15 pound (7·5 kg) pike could not be considered very big, but it will be somewhere in the region of 34 inches (85 cm) long and certainly it will be a giant in comparison with the tiny slips of roach and dace which we have been considering. Such a pike will not be a regular angling occurrence, but neither will it be one of those daydreams and you can, with reality, anticipate a fish of this size turning up when you are pike fishing. In the three weeks leading up to the writing of this section, a friend and I have taken four pike around the 15 pounds (7·5 kg) mark — which should indicate that pike in this weight category are by no means rare.

Ah, I can imagine you might say to yourself, *but this fellow has been fishing for a long time and knows how to do it. What chance have I got?*

I can understand that, but I want you now to consider the case of a young friend of mine, who had never caught a pike before, who was taken to a river to catch one — and ended the day with a fish of 23 pounds (12·5 kg). On another occasion, a newcomer to angling joined me to fish a deep gravel pit, with tackle which I loaned to him. *He* caught a pike of almost 30 pounds (15 kg) — which is a bigger pike than I have ever caught!

As I wrote earlier, angling is one of the few pastimes where you do not have to practise for years to be successful, and if you present a bait in the right manner, the fish which takes that bait does not know whether you have been fishing for four months or forty years!

As a general rule, you can expect to find most of your pike weighing two or three pounds (1 or 1·5 kg), with the odd six or eight-pounder (3 or 4 kg) coming along occasionally – and by roach and dace fishing standards, these pike will seem to be very big. That does not matter, the majority of roach that you catch will weigh merely a few ounces or grams, but that does not stop you from fishing with hopes of a two pound (1 kg) fish in mind. If you concentrate on a water that holds pike – and most waters do – you will probably find it much easier to catch a big pike than you would, say, a big chub or perch.

In angling, 'big' is a relative term, and while a 15 pound (7·5 kg) pike, or carp, may not be considered big in national angling circles, it will still come to you as a very big fish and you will have great difficulty in controlling it on the sort of tackle you have been using for your general fishing.

To enjoy successful pike and carp fishing, you *have* to acquire another, more powerful rod. Fortunately, there are many sensibly designed rods for this aspect – many designed by famous anglers who specialise in catching big fish – and if you tell your tackle dealer what you have in mind, he will have a suitable rod in keeping with what you want to spend.

The line that you use will also have to be powerful, in keeping with the rod and, again, your tackle dealer will tell you what range of lines you can use with a particular rod. I would suggest that, initially, you settle for a 12 pound (6 kg) breaking strain nylon line, which will be sufficiently strong to allow for any errors you may make in playing medium-

Below: a typical set of tackle for pike fishing – consisting of a powerful two-piece rod, fixed-spool reel with a large capacity drum, 12 pound (6 kg) breaking strain line, arlesy bomb and stop, wire trace with a large single hook and two trebles for dead bait. As this is ledger tackle you will also require a pair of rod rests, and to disgorge your fish a gag and pair of large artery forceps or long-nosed pliers. If you are going to keep the pike for the table a priest will also be needed to kill it cleanly. *Painting by Ted Wade of a drawing by Donald Downs.*

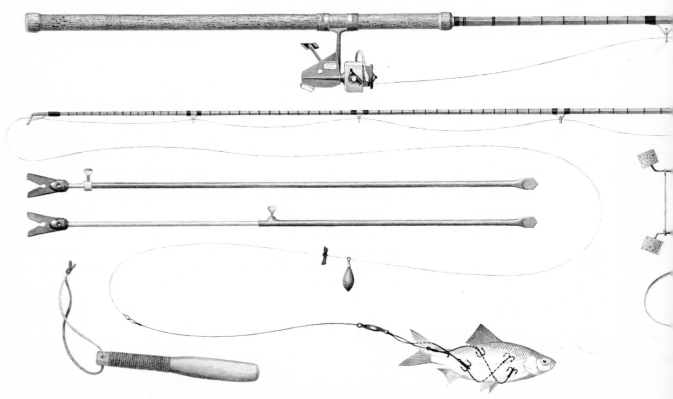

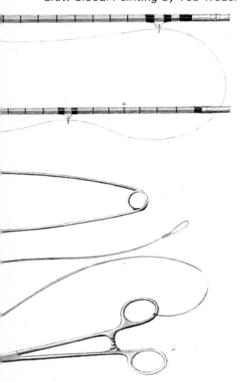

Above: this is the pike — note the streamlined body with powerful fins located to the rear enabling him to propel himself through the water and seize his prey with his distinctive large mouth, full of sharp teeth. Always take great care when removing hooks from a pike's mouth because quite a small one can give a bite that will draw blood. *Painting by Ted Wade.*

sized fish and give you enough power to beat a big one. Later in your angling, you may feel that you want to use a lighter line, and that is quite all right, because we all have our own ideas about what makes for sport in fishing, but if you have been used to catching small fish, that first pike will feel like a sandbag powered by an outboard engine and, where you were once used to swinging your fish into your hand, you may find that you need ten or fifteen minutes before you can get your fish to the landing net.

It is at this stage that you will appreciate having a large net, for even a small pike will stretch right across the small nets you see in use on some waters.

You do not have to buy a new reel to hold the high breaking strain line for your specialist fishing, for all of the well-known brands of reels have large capacity spools, either included with the reel, or readily available. You merely depress the button which holds one spool in place, remove the spool and replace it with another.

Pike are fierce predators and feed upon all manner of creatures, living and dead. Traditionally, the standard pike bait is a live fish, but in comparatively recent years dead fish have been shown to be very effective, and this aspect has been greatly publicised by Fred J. Taylor, a famous English angler and newspaper columnist. Really, I believe, the moral issue rests with the angler involved, but I share Fred J.'s dislike of impaling a small live fish upon treble hooks — although I confess to having used live-baits to catch hundreds of pike between twelve and eighteen pounds (6 and 9 kg).

Spinners, plugs and all kinds of metal lures will also account for pike but, in my experience, the pike tend to be small. I do not say that you *cannot* catch big pike on spoons and plugs, only that I have never managed to catch the larger fish that way. However, it can be very enjoyable to

Right: a smallish pike weighing 3 pound 9 ounces (1·5 kg) still gave pleasure to this young angler. Despite its size it was very necessary to use a wire trace against its teeth and to take great care when removing the spinner.

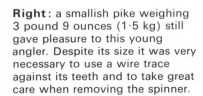

Below: not without reason is the pike sometimes called the fresh-water shark. This veritable giant shown with its captor needed strong tackle and a stout wire trace to bring it to the net.

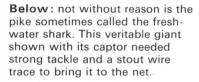

travel lightly along a water course, armed with a spinning rod, a few lures and a landing net; unhindered by the mass of tackle which anglers tend to transport with them.

However you tackle your pike, you must bear in mind that your quarry has exceptionally sharp teeth which can sever nylon line almost immediately on contact. Consequently, you will need a wire trace between the hooks and the nylon. Traces may be acquired ready-made, or you may buy swivels, hooks, and a spool of wire, to make them up yourself — which, of course, is the most inexpensive way.

Trace wire for our purposes is either single strand wire or nylon-coated braided wire. There are opposing schools of thought on which type of wire is superior, but I think that there is nothing to choose between the two. With single strand wire, you have to watch out for kinking, which weakens the wire. With nylon-covered wire, you have to watch for breaks in the nylon coating, where water may enter and cause the wire to rust.

Hooks for pike fishing are normally thought of as brebles, but I have used single hooks to good effect on many occasions and the best fishing I have enjoyed has been when using a single, well-honed number 4 hook whipped carefully to an eight pound (4 kg) breaking strain wire. This produced a catch of seven pike between six and 18 pounds (3 and 9 kg) and another time, a solitary fish of twenty-four pounds (12 kg).

Floats are normally associated with live-baiting, but may also be used to good effect to suspend dead baits above weed in still water or to drift them down on the current in rivers. The traditional float is a split-bung known as a *'Fishing Gazette'* float, where the line slots into a groove in the main body of the float and is jammed in place by a wooden peg. An old-fashioned design, it amazes me that they are still manufactured for, quite apart from the tendency of the cork to split and break up after continuous use, they present tremendous resistance to a live bait towing the float about and sap the power in a strike that has to be made over a long distance.

I have used tube or egg-shaped floats with a line channel right through the centre for many years, and know of nothing to improve upon these. This type of flat has several distinct advantages. You place a stop-knot in the line to stop the float for the depth you wish to fish. The float stays down on the trace swivel for casting — thus keeping weight as close to the end of the line as possible to make casting easier — but once in the water the float moves up the line until it comes against the stop-knot. When you strike, you do not have to overcome the drag of the float before the power of the strike can contact the fish, for the float is not fixed to the line and the power of the strike travels directly *through* the channel in the float.

Nine times out of ten, a pike takes its prey across the body and holds the fish in its jaws for a while before turning it and swallowing. Occasionally, a pike may launch itself from ambush and engulf a fish almost in a long continuous movement, and sometimes it will literally shovel a dead fish from the bottom into its throat. However, for angling purposes we think of pike as holding a bait across its jaws for a time before turning the fish for swallowing, and so you must not strike as soon as the float goes away. Most times, the pike takes your bait and runs for fifteen or twenty yards (15 or 20 m). When the float goes under you should have the reel open so that this run is unimpeded, and you let the line peel off over the spool of the reel unchecked. When the float comes back to the surface and remains stationary, or line stops peeling from the reel with the float still out of sight, you should allow roughly five seconds to pass and then strike firmly.

Using this routine, you will catch quite a few pike — but you will also miss quite a few! You see, like other aspects of angling, pike fishing is not cut-and-dried and, as Richard Walker wrote, the two words that do not apply to angling are 'always' and 'never'.

Sometimes pike will not run with a bait, but merely hold the float down in the water. At other times they may run

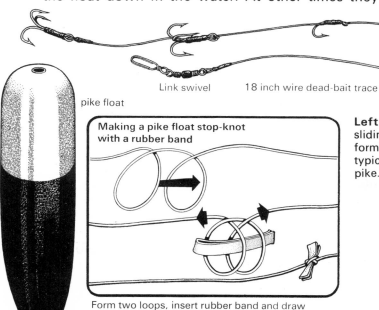

Link swivel   18 inch wire dead-bait trace

pike float

Making a pike float stop-knot with a rubber band

Left: this illustration shows a sliding float, the method of forming a stop on the line, and typical hook and trace rigs for pike.

Form two loops, insert rubber band and draw tight. When in place, trim rubber band to within $\frac{1}{4}$ inch either side

31

away with a bait held across their jaws and not stop to turn it, but just keep on running. Sometimes you strike, by accepted thinking, too soon, and find that the pike has engulfed the bait completely and you cannot reach the hooks. Sometimes you delay the strike a long time, and still find you are pulling baits away from pike which have not turned them. None of this is related to the angler's ability or experience, for pike are not constant in their habits and the routine that hooks them on one day may not hook them on the next. However, the incidents I have mentioned are occasional happenings and most times you will catch pike by letting them run with a bait and striking approximately five seconds after the run stops.

With your first pike on the bank, you will be able to

appreciate the size of its teeth – and if your fish is in the fifteen to twenty pound (7·5 to 10 kg) class, those teeth may be like those of a small dog! Even very small pike will have needle-like teeth which can cut your hands and, while they will not make definite attempts to bite you, they can inflict painful wounds as they thrash around with jaws snapping.

To remove the hooks cleanly and safely, you will need a gag to keep the pike's jaws open and a pair of pliers or long forceps to reach the hooks.

On some waters, anglers are required to kill all pike they catch, but in the normal course of fishing you should not kill pike as a matter of form. Fierce they may well look, and of course they feed upon other fish, but pike, too, have a place in the water world.

Many anglers maintain that pike never allow other fish to grow large in a particular water, and consequently must be removed to give other species a chance to thrive. These anglers seldom pause to consider that the best mixed fisheries in Europe have very big pike and very big fish of other species as well.

Carp can grow as large as pike, but they are a more gentle, benign species, with no call for wire traces and fish baits. There can be little doubt that the carp is one of the most difficult of the anglers quarry, and although there are some gravel-pits dotted about the countryside which have been stocked with hundreds of artificially-reared carp, which tend to fall easily to baits, carp are generally the most discerning of the freshwater species.

Now you would stand little chance with the big floats used in pike fishing, for carp are very wary of resistance and would immediately reject a bait if they felt the buoyancy of a float at the surface. You do, of course, occasionally hook carp when fishing with very light float tackle, but you very seldom land these fish.

Standard carp tackle is virtually the free line rig we have already considered — with a strong hook whipped direct to the line, no float to cause resistance to a taking fish and no leads to catch on obstructions on the bottom when the fish moves off with the bait. Remember, if a carp finds anything suspicious about the bait when it picks it up, it will immediately eject it — and the way to get around this is to keep the tackle as simple, and as strong, as possible. Again, the weight of the bait provides all the weight we need for casting, and — with a correctly filled reel spool — you may be surprised at how far you may cast a piece of crust, ball of bread, or a large lobworm.

Carp will take many baits and, to a certain extent, successful baits tend to be controlled by fashions in the angling world. The largest carp I ever caught — a 27 pounder (13·5 kg), in 1955 — fell for a boiled potato, and during the 1950s potatoes were accepted as standard carp bait. I have caught hundreds of carp between eight and 15 pounds (4 and 7·5 kg), on balls of bread and on large worms, but currently these are considered old-fashioned and the 'in' baits of recent years are mixtures of flour and rusk on a base of tinned cat-food!

33

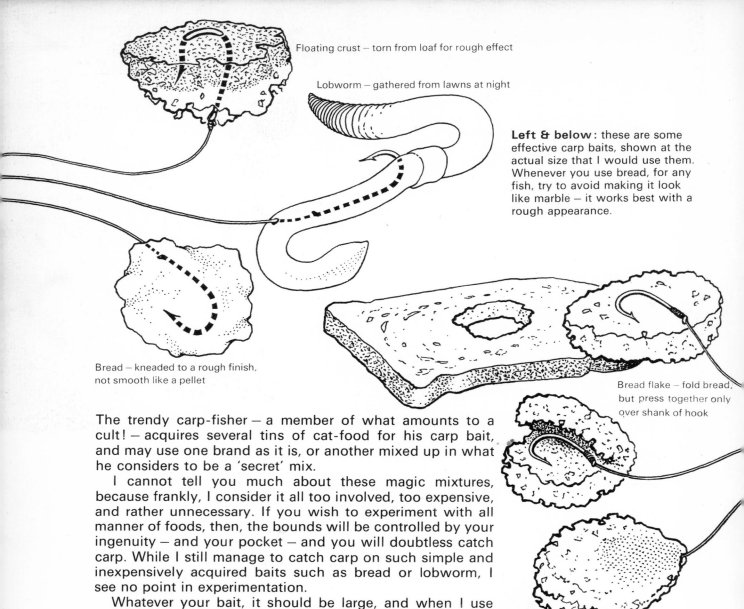

Floating crust — torn from loaf for rough effect

Lobworm — gathered from lawns at night

Left & below: these are some effective carp baits, shown at the actual size that I would use them. Whenever you use bread, for any fish, try to avoid making it look like marble — it works best with a rough appearance.

Bread — kneaded to a rough finish, not smooth like a pellet

Bread flake — fold bread, but press together only over shank of hook

Do not knead or you will destroy the effect of flake. It will expand in water.

The trendy carp-fisher — a member of what amounts to a cult! — acquires several tins of cat-food for his carp bait, and may use one brand as it is, or another mixed up in what he considers to be a 'secret' mix.

I cannot tell you much about these magic mixtures, because frankly, I consider it all too involved, too expensive, and rather unnecessary. If you wish to experiment with all manner of foods, then, the bounds will be controlled by your ingenuity — and your pocket — and you will doubtless catch carp. While I still manage to catch carp on such simple and inexpensively acquired baits such as bread or lobworm, I see no point in experimentation.

Whatever your bait, it should be large, and when I use bread, I fish with a well-kneaded bread-paste lump, roughly the size of a golf ball. This is, of course, specialised fishing and if you were out merely to catch whatever came along, obviously you would use a bait of a size that could be easily picked up by roach, bream, crucian carp, or whatever else happened to be in the area of your bait. In any form of specialised angling, you have to accept that you may not catch any fish at all, but when you do, they tend to be rather large specimens.

Small fish do whittle down large baits and occasionally hook themselves on outstandingly large hooks, but most times you have a good chance of catching carp. It is an all-or-nothing venture, for your large bait is calculated to prevent small fish pestering the bait you intend for carp.

The best time to catch carp depends much upon the nature of the water you are fishing. Most of the time it is summer and autumn fishing, and the best of fishing tends to come when the water is quiet, undisturbed by picnickers or boats.

This, of course, applies to all forms of angling, but while you may often catch species such as roach, perch and bream, when boats are cruising in the vicinity, you will not be able to catch carp under the same conditions.

I would like you to understand that all kinds of fish have been caught on all kinds of improbable baits, at improbable times of the year, and in the most improbable places. In the main, these are freak occurrences and you might fish for many years and never repeat the success. I believe in catching fish consistently, not just once or twice a year, and so I am attempting to provide generalised information that will enable you to catch the kinds of fish I catch, consistently.

On some very good carp waters you have to fish at dawn, or dusk, to catch the fish when they are feeding confidently. On other waters, you can catch your carp only by fishing through the night. A few waters do offer opportunities to catch carp at any time of the day, but these are quiet, undisturbed waters. It is improbable that you will catch a carp which sees you first, and obviously there is little point in your being tucked away safely out of sight if people are walking, or children playing around the water-side.

Imagine the scene of a pool in the country, or some gravel-pit on the outskirts of a town. It has been a very hot day, and people have descended upon the water in their hundreds during the course of that day. People have thrown sticks for prancing dogs, children have sailed their boats and paddled in the shallows, and the carp have withdrawn to the depths far out, or to bask in the sun at the surface. If you look carefully you can see them, like blue-grey torpedoes, lying

Above: fine though these fish are, they are not really big by carp standards. However, even these fish would test your arms and tackle to the utmost, and you see now why I emphasise a powerful rod for this fishing.

Above: the forked top to the rear rod rest should be big enough and wide enough to hold the thickness of the cork handle. Rubber or plastic forks may be bought separately and screwed or pushed onto metal rod supports. Some supports are telescopic and are adjustable, and although this is not absolutely necessary it does have advantages if the banks are hard or stony as it makes it easy to adjust heights.

stationary just below the surface. This is how I have discovered carp in the most public of waters and made plans for how I might catch them during the silent hours.

The sun goes off the water and gradually the number of visitors dwindles and the splashing children make their way home. Now there are just the occasional, quiet strollers, and out in the water the blue-grey shapes begin to stir. Because they are big fish, they need lots of food and they have lain in the sun all day, taking only insects from the surface. Now is the time to attempt to catch them, setting everything in order for the time when the carp will sink to the bed to feed or, with darkness, come right into the shallow margins to see what can be found in the way of food. Having more intelligence than other species of fish, the carp soon realise that food is to be found in areas where people feed the ducks !

At home that afternoon, you will have whipped a number 4 hook direct to your reel line, ensuring that the slippery qualities of nylon were defeated, and daubed your whipping over with nail varnish so that it would remain secure for what might be a powerful tussle. Now, you put the reel onto your big rod, open the bale arm, take hold of the hook and run it through the rod rings. You take a ball of bread and mould it in a large lump about the hook; or a big lobworm, which you thread onto the hook and partially up the line.

The rod swings out smoothly but strongly, and the line peels easily off the reel to drop the bait some 20 yards (20 metres) out in the water. You lay the rod down onto two rests, the leading rest sunk well into the ground so that the rod tip points down towards the water — and check that the reel is open to give line, and that the line may pass unhindered through the rod rings. You take a piece of tinfoil and make a little tube of it about the line between the first and second rod rings, and this hangs down on the line.

Now you settle back to wait, listening to the sounds of the approaching night, almost mesmerised by the foil tube,

willing it to move. All carp fishers have gone through this, and the outcome of this aspect is probably more influenced by luck than any other. I spent countless hours over three seasons beside a beautiful carp lake in Hampshire before a carp fell to my rod. Then I moved to Kent and, within the first ten minutes of fishing a lake I had never seen previously, I hooked a carp of 19½ pounds (10 kg). Carp fishing tends to be a little like that.

When everything goes correctly and a carp taking your bait is indicated by the tinfoil lifting jerkily on the line, you have to act cooly. This is easier said than done, for my nerves still dance at that first indication and I think of a great leviathan somewhere out there in the dark water. However, do not snatch at the rod, but quickly — and without touching the rod or reel — check that the line has not snagged about the rod rest, or reel handle. You have to be quick, for after the jerking twitch the next thing you will be aware of is the foil tube being level with the rod rings, and the line peeling off the reel as the carp runs.

Take position above the rod, put one hand carefully about the rod handle, the other hand to the reel handle and give one turn to close the reel at the same time that you sweep the rod up to set the hook.

What happens next will be startling. You should encounter a seemingly unstoppable force and as the rod bucks and strains, you will hear your slipping clutch screeching as the carp takes line. Do not attempt to wind the handle, just lean back on the rod and let the fish take line under pressure. You turn the handle to retrieve line *only when tension comes off the rod tip* — and stop turning when you hear the sound of the clutch.

As with a pike encounter, this could be a very lengthy battle. Now you have a fish that has to be played out, rather than merely swung in, and the strength of your tackle, and how you handle it, will decide the outcome.

Above: the top to the front rest is usually smaller and narrower but not necessarily — however it must have a slot or groove to enable the line to run through without the rod pressing on it and trapping it. This allows a fish to run for some distance, slipping line off the reel (and also moving the foil tube) without feeling any resistance.

Fixed-Spool Reel

In a book of this nature it is impossible to embrace fully all the vagaries of angling and all the known tackle and technique, for single aspects alone of angling have lengthy books devoted to them. Now, while I have written that there is no such thing as a general-purpose rod, the **fixed-spool reel** could be regarded as a general purpose reel and I would rate it as the most important single item of fishing tackle. Certainly, it is an item to be properly understood, and the better you understand the full use of your tackle, so the better you will eventually fish. The full extent of the use of most items of tackle is immediately obvious, but that of the fixed-spool reel is not, and, in my experience, seventy-five per cent of all anglers fail to use the reel to its full potential.

A versatile reel, the fixed-spool will do anything that can be done with any other design of reel, whether one is considering match fishing, coarse fishing in general, beach-casting for sea fish or spinning for trout and salmon. The reels for different kinds of fishing will vary in size — although some models can be made to suit almost all of these aspects merely by switching to different spools of different line strength — but the technique remains the same for all forms of fishing.

To achieve the effortless, long-distance casting for which this reel was designed, you have to ensure that the spool is filled with line to within 1/16th (1·6 mm) of the lip. The line will not flip easily over the edge of the spool — particularly when using light baits — if it is merely half-filled.

The fish that we catch most of the time are so small that the reel does not come fully into play, and it is merely a case of winding them in. Big fish cannot be treated in such a manner, and no angler ever beat a really big fish in a straight tug-of-war. Line has to be allowed to the powerful lunges of the big fish, and this is done through a **slipping clutch.**

The slipping clutch enables the spool to revolve and give line under tension, and this tension is adjustable either by a wing-type screw nut on the front of the spool, or a milled knob to the rear of the reel. Conventionally, the slipping-clutch is controlled from the front of the reel, but some first class modern reels have a stern clutch, or drag, control.

If you screw the slipping clutch down too hard, then the line cannot come off the spool when the bail arm is closed and a breakage occurs at the point where the pull of the fish exceeds the breaking strain of the line. As you ease off on the slipping clutch, so the line begins to come off easier until it will run to the slightest pull. If you are using five pound (2·5 kg) line and the clutch gives to a pull of three pounds (1·5 kg), then there is no danger of a breakage. You can gauge this by attaching your line to a spring balance once

Above: two reel spools are shown here, the upper spool is not correctly filled with line. When casting with an under-filled spool like this, the line will drag as it is pulled over the front lip of the spool and prevent the free run necessary for a long effortless cast. The lower spool is correctly filled, the line being wound on evenly to within 1/16 of an inch (1·6 mm) of the lip. When the cast is made even the lightest bait will pull the line easily and smoothly over the front lip of the spool.

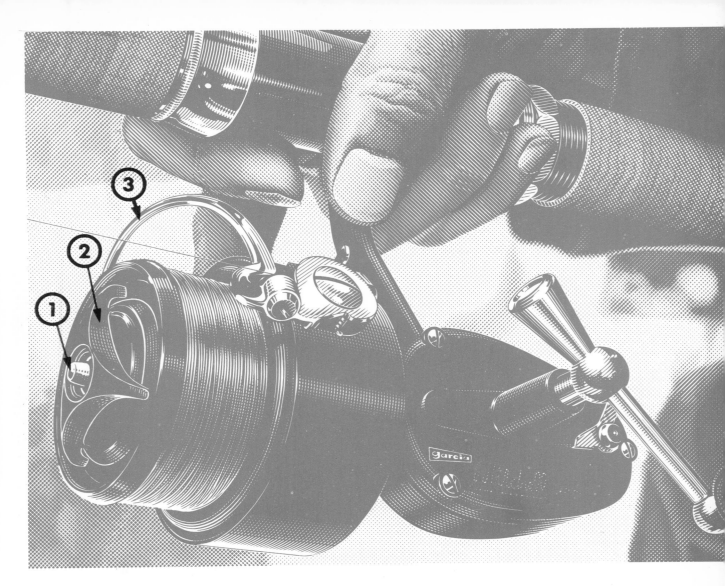

the rod is full rigged, but if you do not have a balance to weigh your fish, then you merely tie your line to some fixed object, flex the rod and adjust the slipping clutch until the reel gives line with the rod fully curved.

When a good fish runs, you just let it take line off the clutch, and if it is running too hard, then, you apply extra tension to the spool with your finger. When a fish does take line through the clutch — which may be noted by an audible ratchet — you cannot retrieve line at the same time, no matter how fast you turn the reel handle. You have to let the fish tire itself by long runs under tension, then as it slows, you stop the spool with your finger, lift up with the rod, quickly lower it and wind in what slack line has been made. You keep on doing this: fighting the fish under tension, pulling it towards you when it slows down and then quickly lowering the rod and retrieving line. This is known as 'pumping', and it is how anglers beat unexpected carp on light tackle, or salmon that plough along a river with immense strength. Learn to use the slipping clutch, for it is the 'safety valve' of the fixed-spool reel.

Above: the complete fixed-spool reel with the spool correctly filled and the reel fitted to the rod handle in the winch fitting. With this make of reel the spool may be simply removed by pressing down the button as at 1 with the index finger while holding it with the thumb and remaining fingers and sliding it forward. At 2 can be seen the wing type of screw nut which may be tightened or slackened to adjust the tension of the slipping clutch. The bale arm at 3 is attached to the rotating portion of the reel, and when winding the line in, this arm is in the position shown here. To cast, the line is caught by the index finger of the hand holding the rod and the bale arm 'turned over' the spool with the other hand, thus leaving the line free to slip off the spool when released by the index finger.

Game Fishing

Above: this is a rainbow trout. It was introduced from America in the 1800s, was slow in becoming established but — due to modern fish-farming methods — is now the mainstay of European trout fishing.

Fishing for trout and salmon is generally termed **game** fishing. **Big-game** fishing is, of course, the pursuit of broadbill, marlin, and similar leviathans in tropical saltwater. Game fishing is generally carried out with flies and lures, but in some instances, normally on small, over-grown streams, wild trout are caught with worms and other baits.

Wild trout is the brown trout native to the U.K., surviving in the steams and rivers in which the species has lived for hundreds of years, despite the hazards of pollution and low water levels. These are the rare fish, most often encountered as small fish going four to the pound or about 125 grams each, but occasionally fiercely predatory and attaining weights in excess of 10 pounds (5 kg). Today, such giants are few and far between, most likely to be caught in the deep lakes of Scotland and Ireland, less commonly in the weir-pools of the Thames.

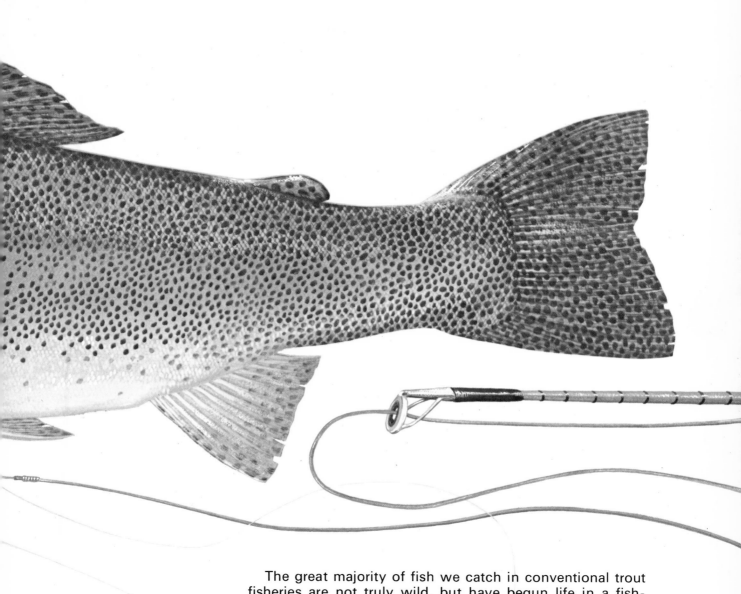

The great majority of fish we catch in conventional trout fisheries are not truly wild, but have begun life in a fish-farmer's stew pond — reared from eggs and cultivated until they reach a size to make them suitable for sport fish, when they are released into lakes, reservoirs and rivers throughout the country.

Some of these cultivated trout *are* brown trout, but the majority are rainbow trout — which grow big very quickly under artificial conditions and thus can conveniently replace the fish taken by anglers on flies and lures. Obviously, most trout taken by anglers are eaten and, as there are very few waters in which trout are able to breed, new stock has to be introduced to the fishery each season. While coarse fish breed prolifically in almost every kind of water and anglers return these fish at the end of the day, there is never in the normal course any need to worry about sufficient stocks.

Most of the expense of trout fishing is because the fish we seek have to be reared artificially before they can be released in waters to provide the quarry for our sport. The situation is akin to that of pheasants and partridges — which would almost certainly become very rare if not re-stocked annually by shooting syndicates.

Pollution prevents salmon from running into many European rivers, but where they do appear, the fishing is very expensive and often booked years in advance. When you consider that it cost a friend of mine — allowing for tackle, travelling and permits — £200 for every salmon he caught during 1973, you will appreciate that these fish are beyond the reach of the majority of young anglers. Sea-trout fishing is also very expensive, mainly because the fish are not widely distributed and you have to travel to remote parts to find them, but good casual fishing may be found in Wales and Ireland.

Those living in salmon-fishing areas will almost certainly have been brought up with a tradition of local methods, and so — because salmon fishing seldom results from the casual "Can I fish, Mister?" approach — I shall keep this section to brown and rainbow trout, which the newcomer to angling could reasonably expect to catch.

Because considerable expense is required to establish and maintain a trout fishery, and to ensure that the method of one angler does not interfere with the sport of another, trout

Left & above: here you can see the special type of vice used to hold the hook in fly-dressing, being demonstrated by John Veniard at the Edenbridge Show. The fly in that vice accounted for the fine trout caught by the 14 year-old boy above. Note the short handle of his fly rod, with the reel sited so that the weight is below the wrist.

anglers are governed by certain rules. The rules vary from fishery to fishery, but generally an angler may take only so many fish above a stipulated size on each visit, and normally the fish must be taken only on artificial flies. Spinning with small lures is allowed on some waters, but this is not common practice and standard technique is fishing with either wet or dry flies. To some it may seem these are unfair restrictions, but it should be kept in mind that this is after all an entirely different kind of angling and so can bring tremendous pleasure and a great sense of achievement. To take a bare hook and dress it with fur and feather so that it looks like a fly or aquatic insect, and then to use it to catch a trout, is the ultimate of the fly-fisher's pleasure.

If you want trout by any means, you must turn to the wooded streams and rough brooks, but if you fancy the comparatively huge, cossetted creatures of still-waters, then, you must abide by the rules governing the fisheries in which they are found.

Artificial flies are made basically of wool, fur, and feathers, held in place with silks and tinsels, although many other materials are used according to the ingenuity of the dresser. Some try to create flies which are exact replicas of a natural insect, while others make almost abstract forms, relying on the colour and movement to attract fish. The fly-dresser may work hundreds of different combinations of materials and colours to devise his own patterns and, just as the artist has his own interpretation of a scene, so the fly-dresser has his own interpretation of how he should simulate, say, a sedge fly, or some other insect. Each pattern has a name, often incorporating that of the originator. Thus we have such

Right: beautiful though they may be, artificial flies are crude by comparison with nature's creations. Two instances are shown here of how the dresser might simulate the real thing, a nymph and a mayfly — one to be fished at the bottom and the other, floating.

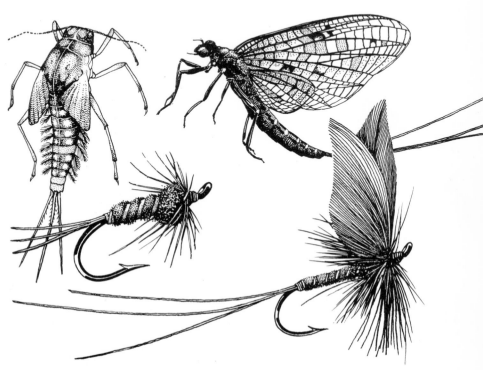

traditionally famous patterns as *Wickham's Fancy*, *Tup's Indispensible*, *Lunn's Particular*, or *Pope's Nondescript*. On the other hand, entertainer Bernard Cribbins is well known on one fishery for his fly called *Bessie Wilton* — dressed with hairs from his pet beagle Bessie, and green wool from his living room carpet!

Flies are dressed either 'wet' or 'dry', depending upon what insect or what stage in the life of an insect, they are supposed to represent. The wet fly is fished below the surface to simulate an aquatic insect or, in some cases, a very small fish. Although anything an angler may use to tempt fish is technically a lure, the larger wet flies — which do not look at all like flies! — are known as **lures**. These may sometimes be two or three inches (5 or 7·5 cm) long, have more than one hook, and are calculated to move through the water like a fish. They are dressed to represent stickle-backs, minnows, roach, or perch, and are most commonly used in reservoirs to catch large rainbow trout.

The dry fly is presented to float on the surface film of the water, suggesting a natural fly which has recently hatched, or has been brought to the water by hazard of flight.

Wet flies are sparsely tied of absorbent materials, with the fibres laying back and the wings close together, almost parallel with the body to allow easy entry and provide convincing movement in the water. Because dry flies have to float, they are tied with resilient hackles to support the hook on the surface film and dressed with materials which do not readily absorb water. The wings are upright and normally spread at a forty-five degree angle to the body.

In other forms of casting we rely upon lead weights to enable us to cast out a bait, but with fly-fishing tackle, there is merely the fly on a length of nylon at the end of the fly line. What you will probably notice, is that the actual fly line is very thick in comparison to conventional fishing line. The weight of the fly is almost negligible, and it would be impossible to cast it any distance if we think of it as we do, say, a leger weight.

Fly Casting

The weight which enables us to cast is in the body of the line itself — distributed over a length of 30 yards (30 m) — and it is the manner in which we move this weight of line, making it roll along itself, that takes the fly out over the water. *For* **fly casting**, *you have to forget the casting you do with a fixed-spool reel* — where you have to swing out a concentrated weight and rely upon its movement to pull line from the spool. We have at one time or another all played with a length of rope, flicking it out so that it snakes forward and rolls along its own length to straighten in front of us. That, basically, is what we do with a fly line, but now, instead of an arm, we use a long spring in the form of a fly rod to bring movement to the line.

When you consider the flexing of a fly rod, you must forget

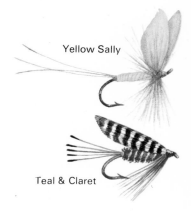

Yellow Sally

Teal & Claret

Above: typical examples of dry fly (1) and wet fly (2). Note the upright wings of 'Yellow Sally'. See how streamlined 'Teal and Claret' is for passage *through* the water.

A

about the type of rod you use for float or leger fishing. That kind of rod is fully flexed only when you are playing a fish, and normally it has to be a fairly big fish to pull the rod over into a full curve. Most of the time, the float or leger rod is rigid, held to feed out line or left laying on rod rests. The fly rod is flexing almost continuously, working with the weight of the line to generate movement to throw the fly forward.

Think of a fly rod as a long and powerful spring, working in conjunction with what — by other fishing standards — is a very thick and heavy line. Before the fly can go forward, the line has to be made to go up high behind us so that its weight will start the rod acting as a spring. In fact, the most important part of fly casting is that backward lift of the line which generates power for the cast.

If the line does not go behind high and uncoil correctly, it will not shoot forward for any distance with accuracy and you will have no control of the line coming down on the water.

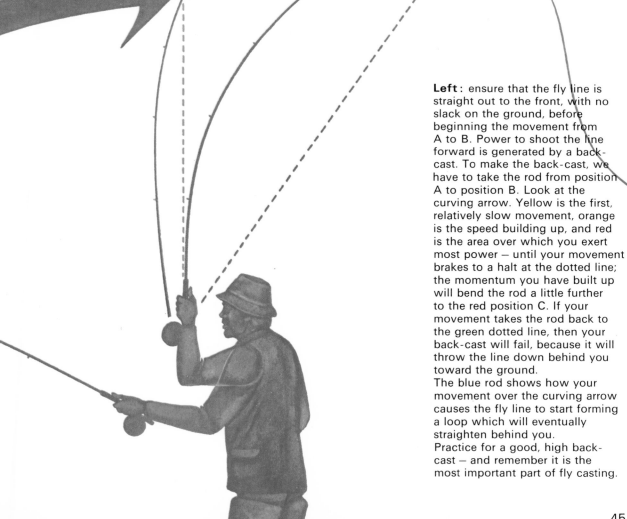

Left: ensure that the fly line is straight out to the front, with no slack on the ground, before beginning the movement from A to B. Power to shoot the line forward is generated by a back-cast. To make the back-cast, we have to take the rod from position A to position B. Look at the curving arrow. Yellow is the first, relatively slow movement, orange is the speed building up, and red is the area over which you exert most power — until your movement brakes to a halt at the dotted line; the momentum you have built up will bend the rod a little further to the red position C. If your movement takes the rod back to the green dotted line, then your back-cast will fail, because it will throw the line down behind you toward the ground.
The blue rod shows how your movement over the curving arrow causes the fly line to start forming a loop which will eventually straighten behind you.
Practice for a good, high back-cast — and remember it is the most important part of fly casting.

As Izaak Walton once remarked on a fishing reel he had never seen, 'It is to be observed better by seeing one of them than by a large demonstration of words.' Look carefully at my drawings here and you will begin to understand how fly casting works.

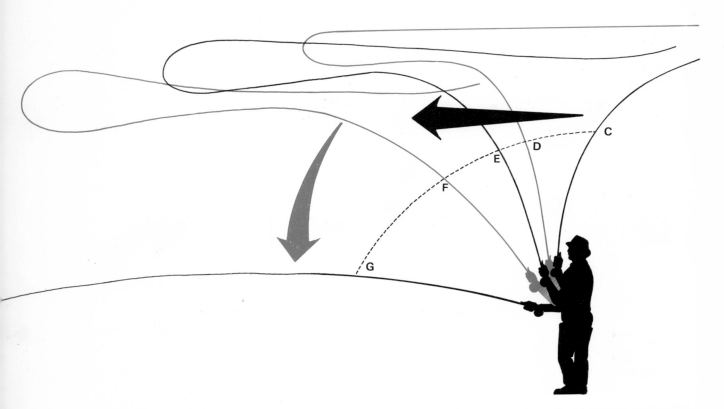

Above: in the backcast, as we saw on the previous page, the line was lifted by the rod going from A to B and finishing in the red position C, with the line straightened out in the air behind you ready to start the forward cast. As shown here this cast is made by flexing the rod sharply forward from C to D which produces the loop that rolls forward.
As the loop extends, the rod follows with diminishing power through positions E and F.
Just before the line straightens out completely the rod is lowered to G allowing the line and fly to fall and land gently on the grass.

If I were with you, we would go out onto a lawn where there were no bushes immediately in front or behind us to entrap the line, or we might go to a park or recreation ground — places where I have taught many friends, who did not have gardens, to cast. We would have with us the rod, reel and line — no flies, for at this stage we are interested only in learning how to make the rod propel the line through the air. I would keep away from concrete or tarmac areas, because our expensive line is plastic-coated and would be badly damaged by abrasions from such rough surfaces. We shall be fishing later with a floating line, but if it were to be chipped and cracked through learning to cast over a rough surface, it would almost certainly sink when we got to the water.

Now we are standing in an open area, with nothing in the vicinity to damage should we get over-enthusiastic in our movements with what amounts to being a very long whip.

I would ask you to take hold of the end of the fly line and run off 25 or 30 feet (750 or 900 cm) and lay the line straight out in front on the grass. Then you stand beside me and I should show you how, by lifting the rod and increasing the speed of my lift until I stop the rod, suddenly, beside my face — the line is lifted from the grass and thrown up high behind us.

We watch the line loop going back and up, getting smaller and smaller as it runs itself out along the length of line, and then, just before the line straightens, I flex the rod forward. Now, the line produces another loop above our heads which travels forward, rolling out along the line until it is straight in front of us. Just before the fly line straightens completely I lower the rod tip and we would expect to see the fly line fall gently onto the grass in an almost straight line. If you are used to casting long distances with a lead weight, I do not doubt that you would be surprised to see that my body did not move to bring impetus to the cast, that it was made almost effortlessly, and that the only movement was in my casting arm, between the elbow and the hand.

With the line placed out to the front on the grass, I would hand you the rod.

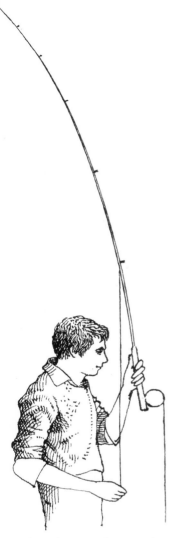

Above: in order to make sure that the rod acts as a strong spring, hold it firmly like this with your thumb straight up the back of the handle and your wrist straight.

Left: an early evening scene on a big water — here an angler casts a nymph with a floating line, hoping to tempt a large trout from this reservoir.

Right & opposite: these pictures show casting demonstrations at game fairs. There you will be able to learn a lot by watching experts and champions and listening to their explanations of just what is happening and why. Even better, at many game fairs and country shows you will find casting tuition given free or for a very reasonable charge. Opposite is a view of Jack Martin showing a perfect roll cast at the Bayfield Game Fair. Jack Martin is a one time British casting champion. For this demonstration he used a chest microphone and so could talk as he demonstrated, which proved most instructive.

You lift the line up from the grass and it starts to go behind nicely, but then it suddenly stops its upward climb and before the line loop can begin to form properly, the fly line falls to the ground in a muddle behind us. Now, this is because you thought that the more you took the rod back, so the better the line would go back, but you had forgotten that I stopped the movement of the rod beside my face. Stopping the rod beside my face ended the *movement* which starts the rod acting as a spring, but because it is a spring, the tip keeps going back to form an arc. Now the power has been generated for the forward cast and the spring, as it were, has been wound up.

You try again, increasing the speed of the rod movement through the quarter-circle over which the rod is moved, until it is stopped, suddenly, beside your face. We turn our

heads to watch, and this time the line goes back and up nicely. You start to flex the rod forward just as the loop is straightening from the fly line, and when that fly line rolls forward in a good cast it seems like the rod has done all the work for you — which, of course, it has!

You try it a few more times, getting the feel of lifting the fly line off the grass slowly and building up the speed of your lift to its peak before stopping the rod vertically. Because you watch the line straightening behind, you begin to appreciate just how long you must pause after stopping the rod vertically before starting it flexing forward. The real power is in the back-cast, there is a pause and, because the rod is sprung with the weight of the line, you use very little effort on the rod to make the forward cast.

My eight year-old son seemed to get the feel of fly-

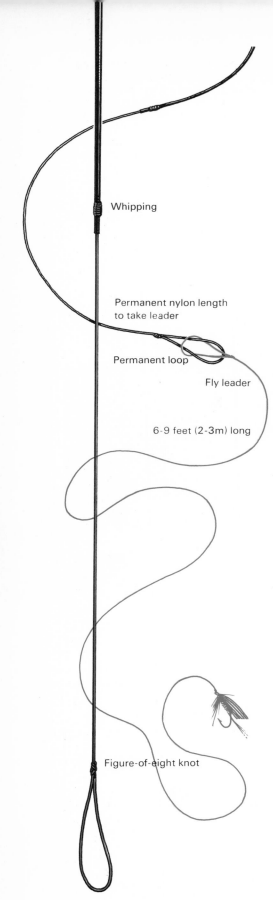

Whipping

Permanent nylon length
to take leader

Permanent loop

Fly leader

6-9 feet (2-3m) long

Figure-of-eight knot

casting instinctively, and often when working in my studio I would hear a slow chant of "Lift — Pause — Push", as he practised on the lawn.

Once you have the feel of it, I would tell you not to throw the line down onto the grass, but to keep it up in the air, with the rod flexing to take it backwards and forwards so that you can truly appreciate the mechanics of it all, and understand the action of the rod. In time, you do not have to turn to watch the line uncoiling behind, but can tell from the movement of the rod exactly when to start the forward cast.

In the past, there has been a tendency to surround fly fishing with all sorts of myths, and even anglers experienced in other aspects of angling have ignored trout fishing because they assumed the casting was very difficult. It should suffice to say that all of my children have been able to cast a pretty good fly from the age of seven years, and one of my daughters won a Ladies Open competition at Olympia when she was nine years old!

Now that you understand the principle of casting, you naturally want to go through the motions of casting as though you were putting an imaginary fly to an imaginary fish. You begin again to lift the line off the grass for the back-cast, but this time, when you drive the rod forward, there comes a sharp, whip-like crack. If you *had* been fishing, that whip-like action would almost certainly have parted the fly from your line.

You have to return to watching the fly line straighten behind, because what you did, was to drive the rod forward too quickly, without allowing sufficient pause for the line loop to uncoil.

As you can see, the build and weight of a fly line is such that if we attached our fly direct to the end, we would find it very difficult to catch fish because of the commotion of the heavy line falling onto the water. To negate this, we attach a **leader** of comparatively fine nylon monofilament to the end of the fly line to take the fly. Traditionally, this length is known as a cast, but as a cast also refers to the throwing of the line, I shall use the American term, leader, to avoid confusion.

The leaders that you buy from your tackle dealer will be tapered, reducing in diameter from beginning to end so that the roll of the fly line passes unchecked along the leader to the fly, and in order to allow the fly to settle on the water with the minimum of commotion. The shorter the leader, the more chance there is of scaring the fish with the fall of the actual fly line, but the longer the leader, so the more difficult it becomes to cast.

If you have access to trout fishing and choose to combine perfecting your casting with attempting to catch fish, I would suggest that you buy a 100 yard (100 m) spool of 5 pound (2·5 kg) breaking strain nylon and cut lengths from this for your casts. Six foot (180 cm) lengths will be ideal to start, and you can extend the length of your leader as your casting progresses. This is the most inexpensive way of making leaders, and also of learning what bad casting technique can do to relatively fine nylon! The ready-made, tapered leaders which you buy from a tackle dealer will normally be nine feet (270 cm) long.

Let us assume your casting is restricted to grass — which will not stop you wanting to see how a fly will turn over at the end of a leader before you get involved with fishing properly. Acquire four or five 'practice' flies. These should be bushy, colourful flies so that you can easily see how they react to your casting, but *before* you start any practice casts, take a pair of pliers and nip off the bend of the hook. This precaution will safeguard other members of the family — especially family pets!

Well, you have your equipment and a fine stock of flies, you understand the casting technique, and you are at last beside the water and raring to catch a trout. What you have to bear in mind now is that all that has gone before is merely the essentials of casting, learned on grass. Once you have made your first attempt, you will find that the line does not lift off as easily — due to the surface friction of the water — as it does from grass, and you will have to allow for this. You will also be able to appreciate graphically what happens when your line falls forward onto the water.

Make for a quiet area of water where there are no snags about — or other anglers! — and try the real thing. Assuming that all goes well you will probably find that the fly does not go as far as you thought it might and it will almost certainly fall to the water with quite a splash.

The first fault is of little consequence, for you will remedy it with experience and technique — and you do not necessarily have to cast a long way to get fish. The second fault *has* to be corrected, for as I have already written you will not catch fish that are frightened, and you should aim to put your fly to a fish so that it appears to be just another item of natural food.

Do not cast your fly down *at* the water, but imagine a point some two feet (60 cm) above the surface and cast there. In that manner, the 'belly' of the fly line will roll over so that the leader falls *onto* the surface, rather than snaking down *into* it. Also, keep your rod tip relatively high as the line rolls out on the forward cast and then, as the line begins to straighten out, lower your rod slowly in keeping with the fall of the line. This will give you the 'feel' of lowering your complete line length, rather than whipping it down at the water.

In my experience, newcomers to fly fishing always worry unduly about the quality of their casting. Do not worry about looking 'professional', just concentrate on placing your fly to catch fish. If you learn to cast so that the line goes out easily, to turn your leader over to drop the fly like gossamer, then, *that* is all you need concern yourself about. There is ample time to learn long-distance casting and it is unwise to become involved with a competitive urge to out-cast your fellow anglers.

Because there are so many types and patterns of artificial

Opposite: this drawing shows a permanent length of 15 or 20 pound (7·5 or 10 kg) breaking strain nylon about 1 foot (30 cm) long which has been fed through the last few millimetres of a fly line and secured with a knot (as shown on page 58). The free end of this length of nylon then has a loop formed in it with a figure-of-eight knot. This enables the leader to be attached and removed as shown, without having to tie knots in the end of the fly line.

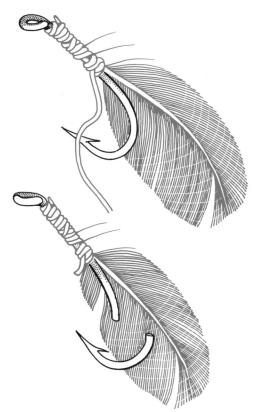

Above: a simple practice fly is shown here — this is made by whipping a small feather firmly onto a hook with a length of cotton or silk and then cutting off the point and barb of the hook at the bend to safeguard spectators — and yourself!

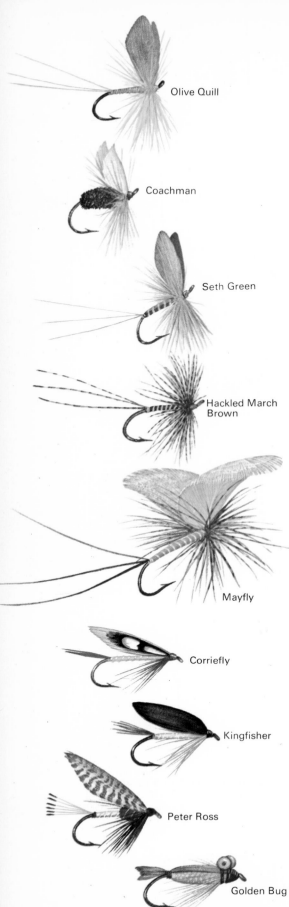

Olive Quill

Coachman

Seth Green

Hackled March Brown

Mayfly

Corriefly

Kingfisher

Peter Ross

Golden Bug

flies, there can be great confusion for the newcomer making a selection — and every angler wants a fly he can feel will almost guarantee to catch fish.

Such a fly exists only in the mind.

Every experienced fly-fisher will have a collection of flies which will enable him to cope with different water situations at different times of the year, and — they hope! — the mood of the trout. If you were to take four elderly and greatly experienced anglers to a particular water, each one would show you a fly which he considered to be the essential trout fly. Each would be different, but they would all catch fish — which should indicate that it is not so much the choice of fly, but what you do with it that counts.

Sometimes — generally in the early summer — trout will take almost anything you cast to them, and at these times they can seem very easy to catch. At other times, the fish seem preoccupied with a certain fly hatching at the time, and then you have to determine what that is and go through your selection of flies to find an artificial one to compare with it in size, shape, and colour. You may never find an exact replica, but you can find something very similar that will fool the trout into seeing your offering as a nymph on the way to the surface to hatch, or as a fly on the surface that has already hatched. In ninety per cent of your fishing, success will depend upon keeping your casting delicate and precise, and making your movements out of sight of the fish.

I have always maintained that I can catch a fish on almost any fly if I can cast it to the fish without it being aware of my presence. Most of the problems in catching fish are set up by the anglers themselves, for their actions in getting a fly to a fish so often cause it to become frightened. The most realistic fly, cast in an exquisite manner, will not tempt a trout that is swimming in fear from a towering shape on the bank. Now, although you may be small in comparison with your friends, you will still appear as a giant to the fish if you stand right on the edge of the water, waving a rod in your hand.

Artificial flies are generally more attractive to anglers than to fish. When you choose your flies, try to imagine how floating flies will look from underneath — as fish see them, or how wet flies will look and move in water. There is no standard advice, and we all tend to pick flies because they look good to *us*, or because we have watched a very successful angler, enquired what pattern he was using, and rushed off and bought some. However, I would suggest a selection of dry flies in dull browns and greys — typically insect colours — and a few contrasting black flies. For wet patterns, the bulk of your choice in dull colours with contrasting tinsel, some with metallic colouring in the body, and a few gaudy, colourful flies that look like nothing that ever lived in water, but will certainly catch fish at times.

Donald Downs, the famous fly-dresser who demonstrates at exhibitions and country fairs all over the British Isles, once tied me some little golden bugs with pop eyes. They were more like cartoon characters than fishing flies, and they were

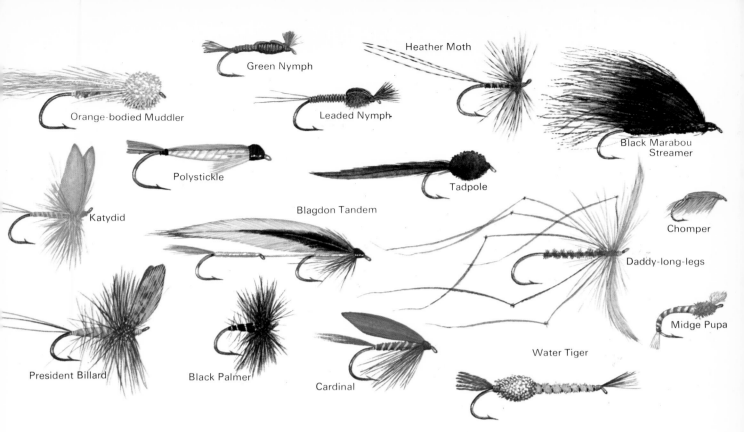

Green Nymph

Heather Moth

Orange-bodied Muddler

Leaded Nymph

Black Marabou Streamer

Polystickle

Tadpole

Katydid

Blagdon Tandem

Chomper

Daddy-long-legs

Midge Pupa

President Billard

Black Palmer

Cardinal

Water Tiger

made for fun — but they so intrigued me that I used them time after time and caught some very big fish with them.

To make up your collection, you could add a few of the large, still water streamers, and some large, bushy white or buff-coloured dry flies. These may be used to advantage on occasions when moths are fluttering along the margins. To complete the collection, you should have some nymphs. These do not look like flies, but simulate the stage before a fly hatches, or some aquatic insect living on or near the bottom. These are always fished beneath the surface, either moving slowly over the bottom or appearing to be swimming to the surface to hatch.

While I will allow for the angler's fancy when choosing a fly, it is good technique which produces fish when using that fly whatever it might be. When fishing dry fly, try to fish from cover and to make the fly fall lightly to the surface — as a fish would expect the natural fly to come down. When using wet fly, retrieve the line so that the fly works in short, jerking movements — as a fish expects to see living forms moving through the water. When fishing a nymph, allow lots of time for the nymph to sink, and then work it back very slowly, inch by inch — as the natural insect would move.

You can never inject *too* much movement — as opposed to speed — into a wet fly, and you can never retrieve a nymph *too* slowly. In fact, trout will even take a stationary fly or nymph, although I would not recommend this sort of fishing as a matter of course, for most of the time it is a sudden, erratic movement that attracts trout away from whatever they are feeding upon at the time.

Opposite & above: these traditional and modern fly patterns are but a few of the many thousands devised for catching trout. Also there are sometimes several variations on a single pattern for example, a May-fly (which is a popular dry fly for June!) may appear completely different from county to county.

Parts of a fly

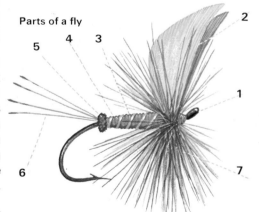

Above: the parts of a fly are as follows: 1 — Eye, 2 — Wings, 3 — Body, 4 — Ribbing, 5 — Butt, 6 — Tail and 7 — Hackle. A fly with the hackle extending along the body — as in President Billard and Black Palmer — is said to be 'Palmered'.

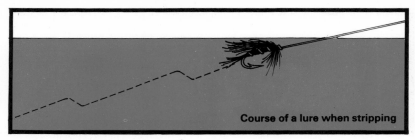

Course of a lure when stripping

Whether fishing wet or dry, always endeavour to fish without making your presence apparent to the fish. On some waters, you have no cover to cast from, and then you have to rely on long-distance casting, but most of the time you can use caution to effect. Do not be fooled into thinking that, because you cannot see the bottom of the water, the fish cannot see you. A stream or a lake may look muddy, but if you take a glass of water you will find there a clarity you did not suspect.

To retrieve sunken flies, you take the line back through the rod rings by hand and not by turning the reel, and this — depending upon how you carry it out — is generally known as 'stripping' or 'bunching'. When stripping, you merely pull the line back in quick jerks, letting the accumulated line fall at your feet or onto the surface of the water. This is normally the routine for fishing big lures or colourful wet flies.

Above: see how this angler has tucked himself up against a tree stump and into the undergrowth. His silhouette is merged with that of the bankside and he still has room to make a reasonable cast. Note, he has the same leg forward as his casting arm.

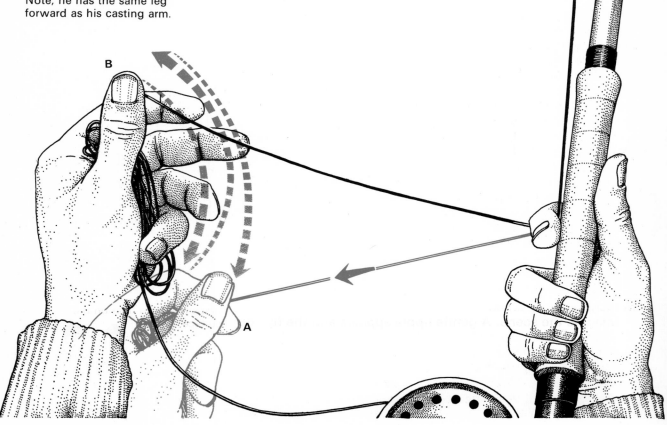

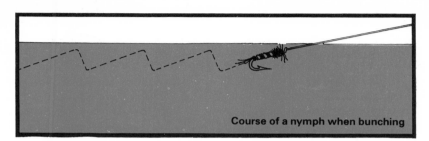

Course of a nymph when bunching

When bunching, you gather or bunch the line in the palm of your hand, using your fingers to gather and retain the line either in loops or figure-of-eight coils. This results in a very slow retrieve and is ideal when fishing small, dull-coloured wet flies or nymphs. Because the waters I fish have heavily wooded banks, I tend to bunch the line so that it is in my hand where I can control it and, on any water, I am inclined to retrieve very slowly; this does not limit the number or the size of fish I take in any way.

Basically, fly lines come in two forms: floating or sinking lines. In the early stages of your fishing, I would recommend a floating line for both your wet and dry fly fishing. When fishing wet fly, your fly sinks only to the depth of the leader and, of course, you will have to consider the length of your leader in relation to the depth of the water you are fishing. The floating tip of the fly line can provide a visual indication of a fish which takes the fly so gently that the movement is not imparted immediately to the rod tip. In the normal course of events, trout will take with a lunge that has an unmistakeable effect upon the rod tip, but sometimes they do take very shyly and then the 'V' marks on the surface from your floating line will let you know that this has happened.

Natural flies on the surface do not normally move in any definite direction, so there is no necessity to retrieve your line in an attempt to make your artificial, dry fly move. You watch for the disturbance of trout rising to natural flies and then cast to drop your artificial fly as accurately as possible. It should lay nicely on the water, with nothing to suggest that it is connected to a line, and then you wait — as patiently as you can — for a trout to come up and take it.

When trout are taking boldly — and particularly when several trout are competing for a small batch of fly, you seldom miss fish then. When you first start fishing, you tend to miss the ones that lie just beneath the surface and 'sip' the fly in. With these fish, you invariably strike too quickly and take the fly away, while by the time you have associated that wild swirl with a fish actually taking your fly, the fish is on the way down again and your strike is just in time — although, in fact, perfectly timed.

Imagine the scene. A gentle ripple appears and the fly you have been watching so intently has suddenly gone. In your excitement you strike, and feel a brief contact before the fish goes free. You are striking too soon.

The fish comes up through the water at the fly, breaks the surface to take it, and then turns to go down again. Ideally, you set your hook as the fish turns down. If you strike as the

Opposite top: shows the course of a wet fly or lure when the line is stripped in. With this method of retrieve the line is gently trapped by the index finger of the right hand (assuming that you hold your rod in your right hand) and lengths of about 1 foot to 1 foot 6 inches (30 cm—45 cm) are pulled in with the left hand. The length of pull and frequency with which it is made will quite obviously make variations to the pattern of the fly's course — but the movement shown here is typical.

Left: shows the pattern made by bunching as described in the illustration opposite below; the movements imparted to the fly are more or less those of a hand's breadth and so give a series of very small slow 'jumps', which are often most realistic and successful for fishing a nymph.

Opposite below: this shows the method of bunching. Hold the line between the finger and thumb with the wrist slightly bent towards the rod at A. Now straighten the wrist and extend the remaining three fingers round the line to gather a short length into the palm at B. Release the grip with the finger and thumb and bend the wrist back to position A to enable you to take another grip and repeat the process, thus gathering line into your hand in loops or coils that will pay out when you shoot line on your next cast.

Below: this illustration shows a typical dry fly. It is tied to represent a natural insect and has a wound herl body that gives the appearance of being segmented. A pair of wings is made from two slips cut from feathers, and the legs are made from a cock's hackle feather that has been wound round the hook shank so that it sticks out (looking something like a chimney sweep's brush) and helps the fly to float on the surface.

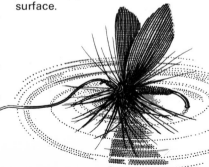

water boils, you may pull the fly clear *before* the fish can take it, or pull the hook free of the fish before it can gain a hold. Make your strike as the fish goes down and then, failing snags in the water, he is almost certainly yours.

If you have to use a very fine nylon leader to fool trout in clear water in summer, bear this in mind when you set the hook. If you strike wildly, you may feel the force of the fish for an instant before the leader parts. A two or three pound (1 or 1·5 kg) breaking strain leader will not stand up to the force exerted by you at one end of the rod and a trout at the other — if you apply that force wildly. Even a two pound (1 kg) trout — which is a fairly standard size on most waters today — may cause that leader to part with a crack like a rifle if the fine nylon has to cope with sudden, excessive force applied in opposite directions. Consider that few fish, regardless of size, break free through sheer strength. *Breakages occur through bad angling technique or tough roots and other snags in the vicinity of a good fish.*

Try to fish with as little slack line on the water as possible at all times, and when the fish takes, strike firmly over a short arc, rather than swing the rod wildly over your shoulder in a great movement.

Regardless of the method of fishing, endeavour to stay out of sight of the fish at all times, kneeling to cast so that your outline against the sky is reduced or, ideally, working in the cover of bankside foliage, bushes and trees. If you cast badly into an area, leave your fly in place for a while, rather than whip the surface with constant casting, and move around in search of fish, exploring the water, rather than stand in one spot and expect fish to come to you.

When you spot a fish, do not start to cast to it immediately, but consider how the prevailing wind may effect your casting and what snags in the water are to be avoided once the fish has taken your fly. By calculating your fishing in this manner, you will catch far more fish than the angler who casts non-stop over a stretch of water.

Basically, that is all you need to know to catch a trout with a fly. There is a great deal of technique and refinement still to be learned, some of which you will still be learning when you have fished for 20 years or more, but the essentials are here. Remember that a trout — although very prettily marked — is merely a fish, with no more intelligence or cunning than any other fish. Remember also, that it responds to danger like any other species of fish and that *you* are its most probable source of danger. If the fish knows that you are there, your chances of catching it are already greatly reduced.

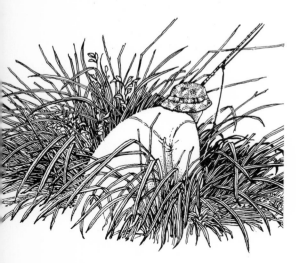

Above: note how the angler has merged himself into the bank in order to drop his fly over a trout that he has crept up on. Absolute stealth should always be observed on the river bank — think of the way a cat stalks and try and be as quiet and as unobtrusive.

Below: the rewards of stalking usually pay off by giving you exciting views of your unsuspecting quarry as illustrated here. The trout is completely unaware that it is being watched. Of course, stealth does not apply to trout fishing only; complete quiet pays dividends in all forms of angling.

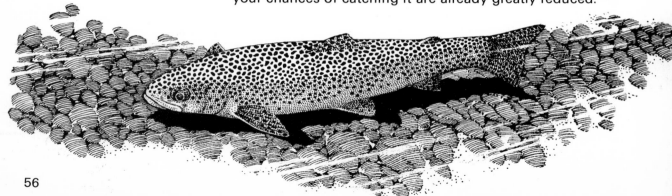

Knots

It is fairly common to find pages full of diagrams for making **knots** in most angling books, with stage by stage drawings of complicated tucks and twists. There are, I suppose, a maximum of 20 or so different knots that are widely written about, but in all the different forms of fishing I do, I don't suppose that I ever use more than five. I am a great believer in simplicity and I do not like the idea of being technical just for the sake of it. As every knot in your tackle link provides a weak point, you should keep those weak points to a minimum. It is well known, of course, that a chain is only as strong as its weakest link, and that is how I consider my tackle from reel to hook.

Before we consider the knots shown here, there are some things you should know about nylon monofilament. Mcst ropes are made up of several thin strands braided together. If one or two of these thin strands break or wear through, the rope can still hold a weight — and will continue to do so until so many of the thin strands have parted that the remainder can no longer hold the strain. I'm sure you must have seen this demonstrated in many suspense films, where the hero hanging from a cliff, struggles to reach the top before the rope that holds him frays to within a single strand!

Right: this illustration shows a half blood knot used for knotting line to swivels and flies.
The line is threaded through the eye at fig 1 and twisted three or four times round itself at fig 2. The free end is then passed through the loop next to the eye and again tucked through itself at fig 3. The knot is then pulled tight, the end trimmed and varnished as shown in fig 4.

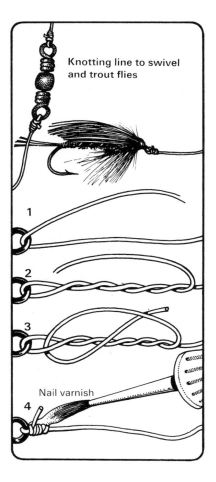

Knotting line to swivel and trout flies

1

2

3

Nail varnish

4

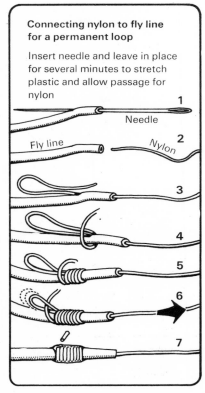

Above: this shows the method of attaching a length of nylon to the end of a fly line (see also page 50).
In fig 1 a hole is made by a needle along the core of the fly line and out through the side. Figs 2 and 3 show the nylon being fed through the hole. (It may be necessary to point or splay the nylon with a sharp knife to ease penetration.) Figs 4 and 5 show a bend of nylon laid along the fly line and turns off the free end of nylon taken along the bend. Fig 6 shows the end of the nylon taken through the loop of the bend on the last turn and then the main length of nylon pulled tight to lock it. Fig 7 shows the surplus end trimmed off and the knot coated with nail varnish.

Nylon monofilament is not made up like that, it is complete as a smooth, single strand. Its strength is in its diameter, or thickness, and when that diameter is damaged — say, by stretching, or through nicks and cuts — then, there is no way of telling what strength it has and exactly when it may break. For example, if you had a brand new spool of 12 pound (6 kg) breaking strain line and this got tangled badly around a reel, suffering nicks and abrasions as you pulled it off, the one-time 12 pound (6 kg) line could part to a pull capable of no more than two pounds (1 kg)!

Always check your line after a tangle, or snagging in bushes, for nicks in its smooth surface. Even if you find slight damage to the line above the float, you should go through the inconvenience of breaking it there and making up the tackle afresh. If you do not, sooner or later you will lose that tackle anyway — and perhaps a good fish with it! The main problem, even in careful fishing, is knots which seem to form miraculously — and particularly in the leader when fly fishing. Carefully remove these knots, or make up fresh tackle, because if your line is going to part under strain, it will part where that knot has formed.

When you buy nylon monofilament, the breaking strain marked on the spool is for the line in its dry state. When you fish, the line absorbs water, and that makes it approximately twenty-five per cent weaker. Even the best sort of knot you can tie will make the line a little weaker, and the more knots you have, the weaker your line becomes. Treat your line with care, use only whatever knots are absolutely necessary, and your line should last you right through a season.

Fish rarely break a line through sheer strength. They normally break lines with the aid of snags in the water — or because it is weak and badly knotted!

Before you form a knot, moisten in your mouth the area of the line to be repaired. When you make the knot, never pull it tight with a jerk. Just pull the knot firmly into place, otherwise you may cause the nylon loops to bite into themselves and make the line much weaker than you believe it to be.

Precautions such as these take a little extra time, and time may seem precious when your friends are rushing to get fishing as quickly as possible. But if you put your tackle together as a strong chain from the reel right through to the hook, you will fare better with landing good fish than any of your friends who think only of getting a float into the water as soon as possible.

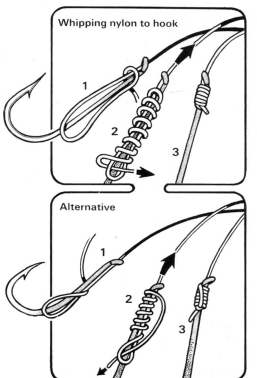

Whipping nylon to hook

1

2

3

Alternative

1

2

3

Left: this shows a suitable knot for attaching nylon to all types of eyed hooks.
Fig 1 shows a bend laid along the hook shank and in fig 2 half a dozen turns of nylon taken along the bend and the free end then passed through the loop. The knot is completed in fig 3 by being drawn tight and the surplus end cut off.
In the alternative below, a loop is formed as shown in fig 1 and the free end wound down towards the eye and then returned and tucked through the loop as in fig 2. The nylon is drawn tight and the end cut off as shown in fig 3.

Right: this illustration shows the figure-of-eight knot used to form the loop in the end of the reel line. Fig 1 shows a bend formed in the end of the nylon and taken back and round itself forming a loop. Fig 2 shows the bend taken through the loop to form the complete knot.
In the lower drawing the hook-to-nylon leader, which is also looped, is attached to the line by being slipped over the loop on the end of the line at fig 1, and the hook end then tucked through the line loop and the leader pulled tight at fig 2.

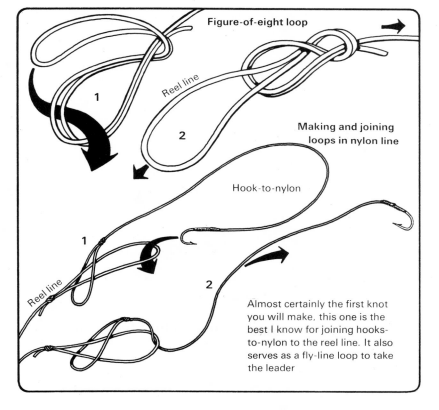

Figure-of-eight loop

Reel line

1

2

Making and joining loops in nylon line

Hook-to-nylon

Reel line

1

2

Almost certainly the first knot you will make, this one is the best I know for joining hooks-to-nylon to the reel line. It also serves as a fly-line loop to take the leader

59

Sea Fishing

I have heard it said that there are two great attractions to **sea fishing**: the first is that there are no restrictions, no private fishing in the sea, the second is that the fish you catch are good to eat. These are undoubted attractions but there are many more, not least of which is the wealth of interest to be found below the tideline for the student of natural history. The fish that you catch *are* good to eat, and if you know only of fish in frozen chunks from a deep-freeze cabinet, then, the flounders that you catch and eventually eat will come as a new and pleasant experience.

There is tremendous scope in sea angling and, like coarse fish angling, tremendous variation in the type of tackle you may use and the type of fish you may catch. At the small end of the range of species there is the mackerel, considered large if it weighs two pounds (1 kg), but very sporting for all

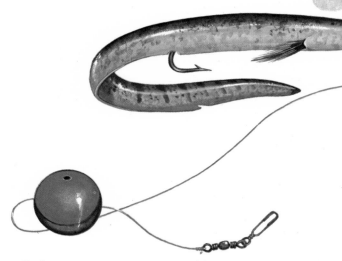

that and capable of providing all the excitement one could want. At the other end of the range are the sharks, sleek blue sharks that haunt the inshore waters where the North Atlantic Drift warms European seas, and great, deep-bodied porbeagles — reaching weights in excess of 300 pounds (150 kg). But I am going to write of sea angling for *you*.

The pursuit of shark fishing can be dangerous — for there is little space on board a small craft to avoid the jaws and lashing tail — and I know of no boats specialising in this form of fishing where anglers under sixteen years are allowed to participate. The charter boats which take groups of anglers out to wrecks and other renowned marks to seek big skate

Above: this is how you would see the flounder through clear water. A bottom-feeding flat-fish, it is mainly found in shallow water and estuaries. Be careful though not to confuse it with the dab which it closely resembles — the flounder has a smooth skin, the dab a rough one. The sand eel is a favourite food of most sea fish and this artificial specimen to the lower left is a particularly handsome fellow.

and conger will not take young anglers unless they are accompanied by an experienced adult, and so I do not intend to denote space here to aspects which are unavailable to most of you at this stage.

We are going to confine our activities to the shoreline, to the simple forms of fishing, where you can go off and spend a few hours in search of fish, just as you would beside some pond or stream.

Those who live close to the sea are the lucky ones, for they may go to the edge of it with the frequency with which we visit our local lake or river. For the rest of us, it is a matter of taking what fishing we can on holidays and weekend excursions to the coast, but before we become involved with

Above: black bream like deep fast water over rocks and come inshore in large shoals in spring and early summer. Their overall colour is deep blackish-blue or purple on the back, fading to silver on the flanks and belly. The dorsal fin is usually the same colour as the back, the other fins are all grey with the exception of the tail fin which is a yellowish grey. Often there are black vertical bars on the upper flank and brown horizontal stripes below the lateral line.

the fish and the fishing, let us consider the tackle we shall need.

Sea angling tends to have an unfortunate association with huge rods and heavy lines, and while some aspects call for such tackle to overcome the rough conditions in which they are used, there is still much sport to be enjoyed with light tackle. I shall assume that you are an all-round angler who has started in coarse fishing — which is the most popular branch of angling — and you have expended all the money you have available. Fine, that should not restrict your fishing, because we are going to adapt some of the tackle we have considered earlier, and if you have to spend any more money, it will be only for small items such as hooks and leads.

The tubular glass rod for your pike and carp fishing will be supple enough to enable you to enjoy good sport with mackerel, and sufficiently strong to beat the occasional large bass that may fall for your bait. The action of this rod will be ideal for casting a bait out to the shingle reaches where plaice and flounder wait, and for playing wrasse which lurk down in the rock cavities. However, it is a lightweight rod and the metal fittings on it will almost certainly be prone to corrosion from saltwater.

Even the spray blown up from the sea on a sunny day can cause corrosion to begin when the rod is put away, so make a point of washing it down with clean, warm tapwater every time you finish fishing.

Your fixed-spool reel, carrying its large capacity spool of 12 pound (6 kg) breaking strain line, also compliments the rod for our kind of sea angling but, again, you must be wary of the effects of saltwater on lightweight metals. Each time you wash down your rod, rub the reel over with a damp cloth,

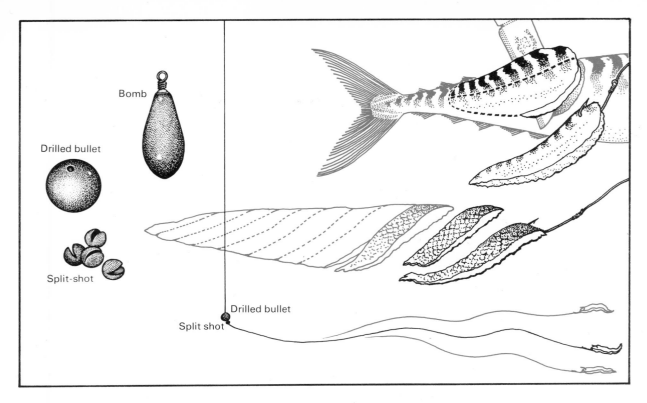

Labels in image: Bomb, Drilled bullet, Split-shot, Drilled bullet, Split shot

and when you fish for long periods, take off the spool, unscrew the handle, and give the reel a thorough washing down.

If you look at nylon line which has been left after extensive fishing in the sea, you will see white, salt crystals encrusted in the coils about the spool. Frankly, I do not know for certain that these crystals cause any drastic weakening of the line, but I do not like to consider it safe enough for big pike or carp fishing afterwards.

Never lay your rod and reel down in soft sand. You may not feel the sandy grit which could penetrate the reel casing at the time, but it could grind away among the gears and eventually ruin your reel. Even when wandering along a beach, I always carry one of the rod rests I use in coarse fishing, and whenever I stop to change a lure or modify the tackle in some way, the rest goes into the sand and the rod goes onto the rest.

All the hooks we use will be whipped direct to the reel line, and the largest hooks we use in freshwater are considered small by sea angling standards. We shall use lures frequently, and the small lures we have used in the past for perch should be ideal for mackerel, with the smaller spoons and lures for pike fishing capable of taking their toll of bass.

The leads you use in freshwater fishing can occasionally be employed for sea angling situations, but you should have some leads between one and one-and-a-half ounces (25 and 40 g) and a good selection of swivels. On rare occasions, I use wire traces for wrasse fishing — these traces withstand the teeth of large wrasse and, unlike nylon, will not part when a good fish lunges underneath jagged rock. Otherwise, we

Above: a piece of mackerel cut from the side makes a very durable bait even in quite turbulent conditions; the best method of cutting and putting on the hook is shown here. A section of fish like this, when used for bait, is known as last or lask.
The method of fishing mackerel last in fast water is to hold the bait down by using a drilled bullet or a bomb, which is stopped from sliding down the line by a split shot. This enables the remaining length of line and the bait to wave enticingly in the current.

just make up different permutations of hooks and leads to suit certain species and prevailing conditions.

Now for the actual fishing. . . .

At the height of summer and into the autumn months, mackerel swarm inshore at most points around the British Isles, and at these times the concentrations of fish may be spotted by splashy commotions in the sea as the mackerel

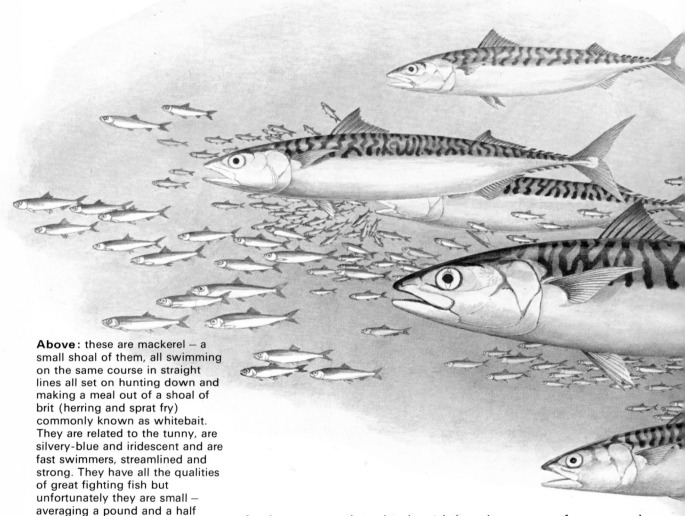

Above: these are mackerel — a small shoal of them, all swimming on the same course in straight lines all set on hunting down and making a meal out of a shoal of brit (herring and sprat fry) commonly known as whitebait. They are related to the tunny, are silvery-blue and iridescent and are fast swimmers, streamlined and strong. They have all the qualities of great fighting fish but unfortunately they are small — averaging a pound and a half (0·6 kg) in weight. They may frequently be caught from the beach when a shoal of whitebait comes close inshore to try and escape them. Then great sport may be had with a fixed-spool reel on a carp or spinning rod, with a small spoon for bait. This 'scaled down' tackle gives a sporting chance to these tough little fish and provides you with the thrill of playing them and not of just winching them out of the water. *Painting by Ted Wade.*

feed upon massing shoals of brit — the young of sprats and herrings, which are served in restaurants as whitebait. There is no mistaking the sign of mackerel attacking the brit shoals, for the commotion is such that, contrasting in an area of flat calm, there appears to be a miniature storm with the surface being lashed to a frenzy.

This can occur at varying distances from the shoreline and the activity is sometimes too far away for the angler to take advantage, unless he is fishing from a boat. However, sometimes it may happen close-in to rocks, and on several occasions I have picked up small fish which have leapt out of the water to avoid the attacks of the mackerel. It frequently occurs well within casting range of the angler with a correctly-filled, fixed-spool reel!

I have a fairly standard routine for catching mackerel, which is a very pleasing way of fishing and capable of bringing superlative sport, by any standards. On a hot summer day, I will change into shorts and an old pair of plimsolls, wear a cap or hat to shade my eyes against the sun, and carry a light shirt to avoid the risk of sunburn. The latter is a wise precaution, because you can stop after hours of exciting fishing and discover, painfully, that the sun has burned your arms and shoulders a deep shade of red.

My tackle is a carp rod, with fixed-spool reel and a small spinning lure, such as a Mepps spoon, or a very good Swedish spinner, the 'Droppen'. I shall have a shoulder bag with me — to hold the fish — and a few alternative lures, such as 'Reflex' or 'Sonette' spinners. Sonette spinners are made with projections on the revolving blade which reputedly cause vibrations attractive to predatory fish and, while I cannot say whether or not this is so, they do seem to account for a lot of fish.

My procedure is to walk casually along the shore, keeping a good eye out to sea for the disturbance that tells me makerel are working in the area. In fact, very little time is spent actually fishing, but the little time that *is* spent fishing is normally very productive.

I may have to walk half-a-mile (800 m) through holiday-makers and past sea-side carnivals before I see what I am looking for — that tell-tale whipping up of the surface which can go unnoticed by hundreds of people along a stretch of beach. Once I get to an area that puts me as close to the commotion as possible — to save casting an unnecessarily long distance, I wade out into the sea. Although paddling on such a day is a pleasant pastime, I do not wade for the fun of it, but to *ensure* that my casting activities with a three-pronged lure do not cause any injury to sun-bathers, or children splashing about on the tide line.

Perhaps surprisingly, you often see great shoals of mackerel just below the surface within thirty or forty yards (30 or 40 m) of where people are enjoying themselves on a beach. In getting into the water to consider their safety, you must also consider your own.

Do not walk into any water where you cannot see the bottom, and do not wade over a bottom made up of large boulders. If you keep to sloping, sandy beaches you should be all right, but do not take any chances on getting out of your depth.

I will make my first cast to the centre of the commotion, quickly engage the reel and begin to retrieve line before the lure can drop too low in the water. Before the lure travels ten feet (300 cm) there will be a savage tug at the rod, and I will not have to strike because the mackerel will have struck the lure so hard that it will have hooked itself. I will play it back, but not without effort, for this lightweight

Below: leads come in many shapes and sizes to suit specific purposes. 1, 2 and 3 are particularly suited by their shape to being cast with a beachcaster rod — 3 has wires projecting which anchor it to the bottom in rough conditions or when a fast tide is running. 4 and 5 are designed to lay firmly on the bottom and their shape is not so suitable for casting but reasonable for being fished from a boat. 6, 7 and 8 are ideal for leger or mid-water fishing (the last as described on page 63). 9 is a Wye lead and is designed for spinning, (as described on page 67).

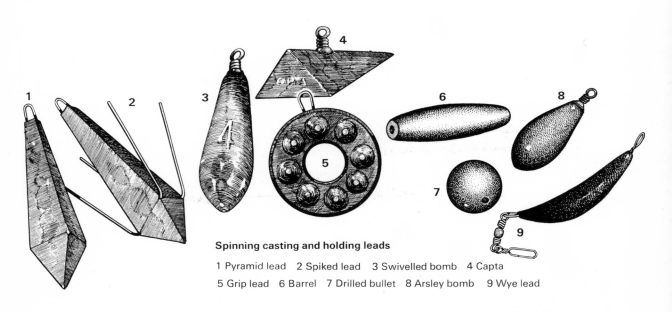

Spinning casting and holding leads

1 Pyramid lead   2 Spiked lead   3 Swivelled bomb   4 Capta
5 Grip lead   6 Barrel   7 Drilled bullet   8 Arsley bomb   9 Wye lead

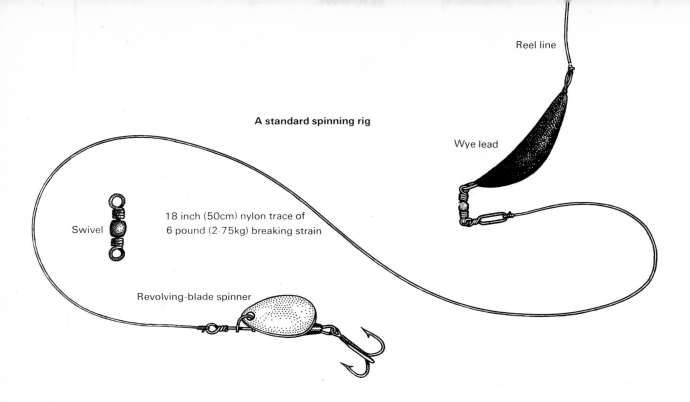

A standard spinning rig

Reel line

Wye lead

Swivel

18 inch (50cm) nylon trace of
6 pound (2·75kg) breaking strain

Revolving-blade spinner

sporting fish plunges with tenacity, or leaps from the water in an explosion of spray. Sometimes it tail-walks across the surface, just like giant marlin do in those films of fishing in tropical seas. Small though mackerel are, they provide the most exciting sport.

Because mackerel make such good eating, I will knock my catch over the head with the pliers I use for removing hooks and pop it into a shoulder bag. I shall do the same with three or four more and then, with sufficient for the table, I shall unhook the others I catch and return them to the sea.

Fishing quickly and accurately, I should be able to take seven or eight fish before the shoal moves on — and so should you, for it really is as easy as that. You do not have to cast at one fish in this form of fishing, but into a broad area in which as many as two hundred mackerel may be concentrated, and it provides a splendid opportunity to improve your casting and to get the feel of the rod and reel. It is improbable that any other kind of fishing will provide you with such hectic activity and so many fish.

When you do find those mackerel shoals, don't be fooled into thinking that this harvest of the sea is unending. By all means enjoy catching twenty or thirty fish, but do not keep more than your family can use and return the others. Too many newcomers to angling get carried away with this sort of fishing and leave piles of fish to rot on the beach.

Once fish cease to fall to your spinner, move on along the beach to track down the movement of the shoal, or to contact new shoals that have moved inshore.

Just as mackerel follow the brit shoals, so bass follow the mackerel shoals, waiting on the fringes to take mackerel

Above: this illustration shows a standard spinning rig — the bait being a revolving blade spinner with a nylon trace. A swivel may be included in the trace to minimise the possibility of kinking from either the movement of the spinner or of a fish when being played. A Wye lead is also incorporated to prevent any kinking being transferred up the line. This lead is made so that all the weight is to the underside (like a ship's keel or a fish's belly) and this stops any twisting. Always fix the reel line to the wire loop of the lead and the spinning trace to the clipped swivel. If you get a Wye lead that has only two wire loops then a swivel can easily be attached with a split ring.

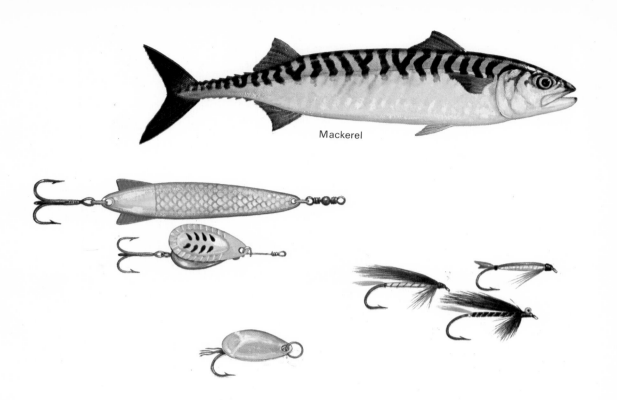

Mackerel

Above: illustrated is a typical selection of lures for mackerel: any small shiny spoons or spinners trolled slowly behind a boat will catch them. When you become more competent, try casting with a light spinning rod. Small feathers and lure-type flies are also very effective for mackerel.

unawares, preferring a large meal to the trouble of catching lots of tiny brit. Sometimes, when you are catching mackerel after mackerel, there comes a tremendous thump on the rod tip, a seemingly unstoppable force — and then your fish is lost. Normally, when this happens, it is because the slipping-clutch on your reel is screwed down too hard and you had not expected a big fish. Unfortunately, the bass that wait on the edge of mackerel shoals are normally the big ones, the nine, 10, or 12 pounders (4·5, 5 or 6 kg) which come rarely in a lifetime of fishing.

The lesson here? Adjust the slipping-clutch so that it does not give line to such fish as mackerel, but make sure that the clutch will slip *before* a strain greater than the breaking strain of your line is put upon it.

In normal fishing for bass, you should search out the areas around pier supports and along harbour walls, or just beyond the edge of the tide, where the surf throws back sand and shingle and disturbs lots of food items for the bass.

You can catch bass by spinning methodically through an area, but these fish do like to stay beside rocks and pilings and your casting has to be good if you are to search out these spots with a spinner. It is much easier to use float tackle, or rolling leger — with ragworm, lugworm, or squid for bait. These baits are generally available from tackle dealers in seaside areas, but you will almost certainly have to book your bait well in advance in popular places at the peak of the season.

Normally, sea angling on holiday is a family pastime and if dad fishes, there should be no problems. If you buy a weekly

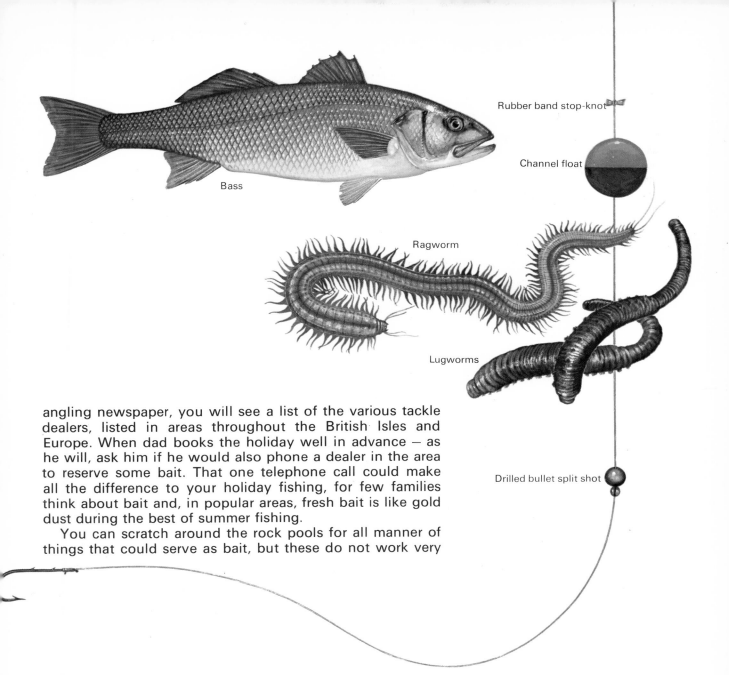

Bass

Rubber band stop-knot

Channel float

Ragworm

Lugworms

Drilled bullet split shot

angling newspaper, you will see a list of the various tackle dealers, listed in areas throughout the British Isles and Europe. When dad books the holiday well in advance — as he will, ask him if he would also phone a dealer in the area to reserve some bait. That one telephone call could make all the difference to your holiday fishing, for few families think about bait and, in popular areas, fresh bait is like gold dust during the best of summer fishing.

You can scratch around the rock pools for all manner of things that could serve as bait, but these do not work very effectively and you lose a lot of fishing time in trying to find something with which to fish. Marine worms — lug and rag — are your best bet, with squid cuttings making the best alternative.

Generally, the best fishing times are when the tide is right up, on its way up, or just going out. Thus, sea anglers tend to think of fishing 'an hour either side of high tide'. Good tackle dealers in the locale will often tell you the places which offer best chances of fish and the best times to try for them.

Where sand and shingle beaches slope far out, you should have a good chance of catching flounder. There are two things in favour of this method of fishing; it is fairly easy and you do not have to rely too much upon the state of the tide to get fish. I have caught some nice flounder in harbour

Above: for bass, rag or lug worms are two of the most effective baits. From surf beaches these should be fished leger style on a surf casting rod, or from rocky areas or headlands a sliding float rig, as illustrated, is favoured to keep your bait just off the rocky sea bed. Spinning from the rocks can at times also be effective, using slightly larger spinners or spoons than those used for mackerel.

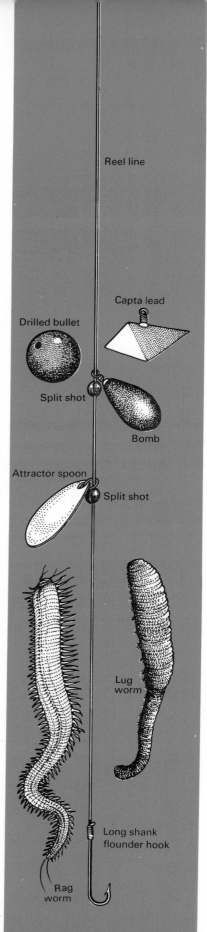

Reel line

Capta lead

Drilled bullet

Split shot

Bomb

Attractor spoon

Split shot

Lug worm

Long shank flounder hook

Rag worm

mouths, and through walking out over the sand to fish in the sea even when the tide is right out. Ragworms are the best bait now, but if you cannot get these, large earthworms can be very effective.

When you fish at low tide, always watch for the tide coming in, and be particularly careful of gullies in the sand behind you, which can fill with water as the tide comes in and cut off your way back!

Because flounder are flat-fish and spend their lives on the sea bed, you obviously have to fish your bait there, and for this, our rolling leger technique is almost unbeatable. When the tide is in, the movement of the sea will keep tackle moving over the sand and, even if it does not roll close to flounder — or plaice — the movement will attract fish to the bait.

When there are lots of fish in an area, the best method is to hold the rod so that you can keep in contact with the weight of the lead. Whenever the line goes slack, you take a few turns carefully on the reel handle until you feel the weight again.

Strike if you feel a sudden sharp tug when turning the handle, for you may have imported enough movement to the bait to cause a bass, or some other fish, to streak at it.

Flounder and plaice have very small mouths and so they need a little time to engulf the bait. When these fish take the worm, you normally feel a series of tremors or a quick, jag-jag-jag movement and you should not strike immediately. Allow a little time to enable the fish to engulf the worm and the hook and then strike with a firm, upward sweep.

In any kind of water, you will never find fish spread around evenly like currants in a cake. Fish concentrate in particular areas because these offer shelter or food, or a combination of both. The so-called 'hot spots' which produce fish after fish, come about when an angler — either by accident or design — discovers an area that holds all the things fish find good. Then, he has only to get his bait into the right place every time and he is almost guaranteed fish.

Flounder, and many other flat-fish, like mud and shingle areas where there are lots of marine worms and shellfish of one sort or another. Obviously, there would be little food for them if they stayed over shingle which was scoured clean by the strong tide, and so they congregate in depressions in the bed and on the sheltered side of sand banks, where sediment and all kinds of food settle, and small marine creatures may thrive without having to compete with the strength of the tide.

If these sheltered points and depressions are very deep, then you could find all kinds of fish in them. Some will have come in for the shelter and food, others will have followed them in to hunt *them* as food. These sort of deep, close-in situations are very rare, and normally you find them off-shore, well beyond casting range, and then only with the aid of a good local boatman who knows the sea coast well.

However the shape and the marvellous automatic camouflage of the flounder, which is able to quickly change colour to blend with its background, does not need deep water to offer security. Most of the time, this fish lies with almost all of its body buried under sand — with only its eyes protruding, alert for food, or danger. Where the bed does not allow the flounder to burrow, its body just takes on the colour of the bed and you have to have keen eyes indeed, to spot a fish that blends perfectly into the background. You see, there is no such thing as a standard colour for flounder, but they are often prettily patterned on top and the bottom side is usually silvery or yellowish.

This is all to our advantage, for the narrow gully close-in to the beach which cannot shelter round fish, like bass, because it has little depth and no rocks or weeds for shelter, can well hold a lot of flounder.

When the tide is right out, you can spot some of the areas that might hold flat-fish when the sea is in. Look for broad gullies where the sand or shingle on either side give way to mud, and the deep slopes which may occur beside the old wooden breakwaters that stretch out along the beach on many coasts. Most of the time you have to rely upon local anglers, boatmen, or beachcombers to tell you where the best spots are, but — as a complete stranger to a shore — I have caught some nice flounder by looking out for the kinds of places I have mentioned and by coming back to fish them when the tide came in.

Watch your footing in mud, and never take chances in areas where you may be cut off from solid land by the sea — even though it may be tempting to stay on for 'just one more cast'.

The type of shoreline you are fishing will control to a great extent, the type of fish you can expect to catch. Bass

Opposite: small rag or lug worms are undoubtedly the finest bait for plaice, flounders or dabs, and the rig illustrated is the best to use during neap tides or slack water. All these flat-fish can provide good sport on a light outfit, but it is important to use as light a lead as possible to hold on the sea bed. With the rig you can use any of the three types of lead shown. The flat capta lead will hold your bait in one spot, while the bomb will permit a little movement. The pierced bullet lead is ideal for shallow water casting where it can roll along the sand and search the sea bed for you. The attractor spoon as shown is not essential, but at times can be most effective.

Below: this illustration shows a typical headland with fish feeding in the vicinity. The gulls are feeding on bait or whitebait, being chased to the surface by mackerel, while below large bass are in turn pursuing the mackerel. The rocky ground around the headland will probably hold wrasse, small conger eels, and bass; while dabs, plaice, and flounders should be found on the sand outside.

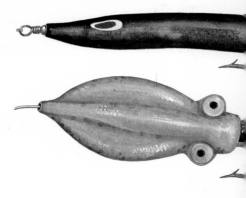

and mackerel can be found in all sorts of situations, but just as flounder and other flat-fish tend to like areas of sloping sand and shingle, so some fish like rocks inshore, which offer shelter and the tiny fish they feed upon. Some coastlines that seem barren and rugged, with waves breaking onto rocks like miniature cliffs, may offer pollack and many will provide an opportunity for wrasse.

These fish may be encountered at all levels in the sea, but almost always are found close to submerged rock faces; from which they dart to take food washed in by the current. They take a bait in a very positive manner and there is seldom any difficulty in hooking them, but to do so we will have to change our method of fishing. We need to fish over snaggy rocks, with the tackle being buffeted back and forth, and a lead on the bottom to catch hard in a crevice. Also, we want to be able to fish the bait at different depths and to keep it close-in to the rock formations. Float tackle is best for this purpose now, as it enables us to fish the bait at various depths until we can find the depth which brings fish, and the sea drives the float around to keep the bait moving. Pollack and wrasse seem to find it hard to resist biting almost anything that moves!

Pollack are generally found out at sea, although some areas lend themselves to shore fishing for this fish. Inshore, you can run nylon straight to the hook and fish conventional float tackle, while out at sea you dispense with the float, use a lead, but hold the rod all the time and try to keep the lead out of the rocks. Fishing from a boat in this manner is normally carried out over fairly deep water, and the most fish fall to the angler who keeps jigging his rod up and down to impart movement to his bait, or lure. Now you can use rubber lures, or strips cut from herring and mackerel.

For wrasse fishing, I do not run the nylon straight to the hook but tie in a wire trace of approximately 24 inches (60 cm) to the hook. This is because a large wrasse has many large, sharp teeth and I have lost fish in the past when they bit through nylon line. Also, when you hook a good wrasse, it does its utmost to get under rock ledges and if there is a gap in the rocks, it will endeavour to dart through it. With a strong fish, this sort of tussle can go on for quite a while and nylon line can be subjected to scraping across jagged rock until it parts. Two feet (60 cm) of wire trace can avoid this (though not always) because you have added protection right above the fish when it is thrusting head-first against rocks and under ledges.

You do not *have* to use the wire trace, and when an area abounds with small wrasse, then you can whip them out quite easily on float tackle where the hook is tied direct to the nylon line. However, we all want to catch a big fish, or bigger fish, and when this fish does come along to take your bait it is a pity to lose it to the cutting edge of a rock.

But surely you don't set out to catch big fish all the time? Quite frankly, I do. I do not always hook them, of course, but *when* I do, I am using the sort of tackle that gives me the best chance of landing them.

Above, right and below: here we show some of the baits that may be used for wrasse or pollack. For fishing rocky coastlines and ledges loved by large wrasse or small pollack, a strip from the flank of a mackerel is an excellent bait and can be fished equally well on float or ledger tackle. When boat fishing over rocks in deep water for these fish live sand-eel, when it can be obtained, is by far the best bait; but if this is not available a small natural squid is an excellent substitute, or the artificial sand-eel called a redgill.

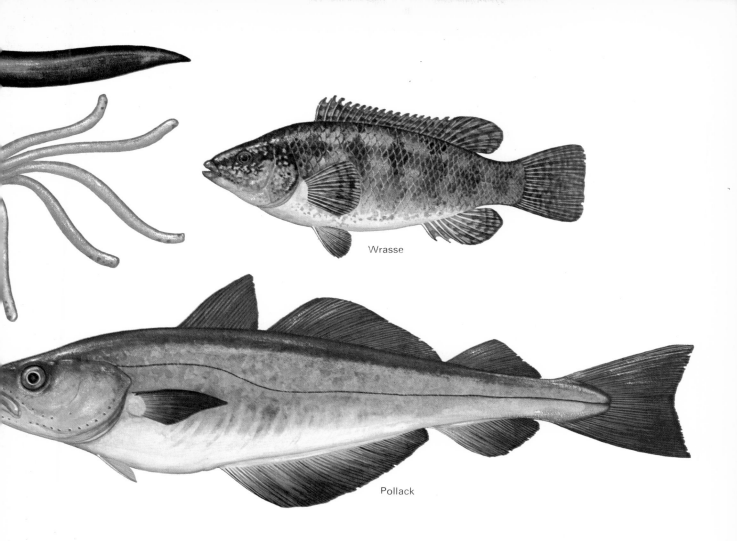

Wrasse

Pollack

Do *not* wear your normal shoes for this fishing, nor plimsolls or bumpers where slippery weed covers smooth rocks. Obviously, you will have to use some common sense about the footwear that will offer you the most security on rocks, according to the nature of the rock surface. Some may be coarse and jagged, others may be smooth and very slippery. *Accidents on rocks beside the sea can cause nasty cuts to hands and knees or, still worse, land you in the water. Then, there is the added danger of the sea washing you against the rocks.*

Just as you have to watch out for the tide when fishing from the beach, you must also keep a sharp lookout when rock fishing. There is a great temptation to fish from the highest rocks, and few of us can resist clambering over small rocks to sit atop a great boulder which juts out into the sea. That is fine when the water is low, but beware of the tide coming in and trapping you on a rock 'island'. Also, remember that you are on a rough and uneven footing over rocks, and be careful how you tread — particularly during the excitement of playing a fish.

Sea angling need not be dangerous — unless you forget that it can be!

There is a limit to what I have been able to show you in this book, for in the hundreds of years since anglers have been writing books on angling, no one has ever written a *complete* guide to angling. A lot of the success in angling depends upon common sense and applying what you read to the different water situations you encounter from day to day and from place to place. However, what I have given you here is the framework upon which you can build your knowledge, and you should be able to go out tomorrow and catch fish of one sort or another.

As you gain experience, you may want to specialise in one form of fishing, or learn about a particular aspect, if so you will find that there are many specialist books from which to choose. The following books I mention are based on the long experience of the authors involved – all of them anglers – and you will gain much from them.

A Guide to Coarse Fishing – written by Peter Stone, and published by Brockhampton Press. *One Hundred and One Fishing Tips* – compiled by Fred J. Taylor and published by the International Publishing Corporation. *Successful Roach Fishing* – my own book, published by David & Charles. *Modern Fly-tying Techniques* – by John Veniard and Donald Downs, published by Adam & Charles Black. *Small Stream & Rough River Fishing* – also written by me, published by Cassell. *Fishing Tackle* – by Dick Orton, a 'Leisure-Plan' book published by The Hamlyn Publishing Group. *Inshore Dinghy Fishing* – by E. J. F. Wood, a 'Leisure-Plan' book published by The Hamlyn Publishing Group. *Successful Sea Angling* – another of my books published by David & Charles.

For the older newcomer to angling, there are two classics which should not be missed: *Angling in Ernest* – by Fred J. Taylor, published by Macdonald, and *Still-water Angling* – by Richard Walker, published by David & Charles.

Those who wish to keep up with what is happening in angling, and to read about the catches in the British Isles each week, will find the latest news in two weekly newspapers: *Angling Times* and *Angler's Mail.* Both these newspapers have sections devoted to the newcomer to angling. There are two monthly publications that cater for the more advanced angler – *Angling,* which covers all aspects of angling, and *Trout & Salmon* which, as the name suggests, is devoted to game fishing and fly-fishing techniques.

Angling has been somewhat neglected in terms of records and statistics, and the only book of this nature, providing details of angling matches back to the early 1900s and record catches for sea and freshwater fish at home and abroad, is *The Woodbine Angling Yearbook.* This is compiled by Colin Graham and published by Queen Anne Press. For details of fish themselves, I know of no publication to beat *Collins Guide to the Freshwater Fishes of Britain & Europe,* by Muus and Dahlstrom, published by Collins. For saltwater, *The Sea Angler's Fishes* – by Michael Kennedy, published by Stanley Paul.

These should form the nucleus of the angler's library.

Opposite: reading about angling can be almost as fascinating as actually taking part in it, and many wonderful books have been written on this subject over the past 500 years. This is one of the earliest advertisements for fishing tackle, published in *The True Art of Angling,* 1744.

Above: this is a picture of Izaak Walton who wrote a famous book about angling which was first published in 1653. It was called *The Compleat Angler*, was very popular and copies are still being published today. Of course, it is published now more out of interest than as a text book on fishing, because tackle and methods have changed enormously and many more things have been discovered about fish; however you may find it interesting to read to see just how much things have changed. Your local library will always get a copy for you. The style is very different from today's writing – but if you can get used to it, it is a fascinating and enjoyable book.

To all Lovers of Angling.
ONESIMUS USTONSON,
Successor to the late Mr. JOHN HERRO, at the

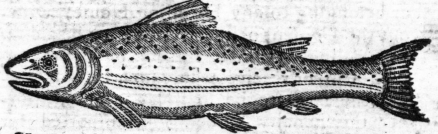

No. 48, the Bottom of Bell-Yard, Temple-Bar,
MAKES all Sorts of Fishing Rods, and all Manner of
the best Fishing Tackle, Wholesale and Retail, at
the lowest Rates; sells the right KIRBY's Hooks, being
the best tempered of any made, which cannot be had at
any other Shop; the best Sort of Artificial Flies, Menow-
Tackle, Jack and Perch, and Artificial Menows; and all
Sorts of Artificial Baits, &c. made upon the said Hooks,
in the neatest Manner, for Pike, Salmon and Trout;
Spring Snap Hooks; Live and Dead Snap, and Live Bait-
Hooks, Trowling Hooks of various Sorts; the best Sort of
Treble and Double Box, and Single Swivels; Gimp, both
Silver and Gold; the best and freshest India Weed or Grass,
just come over; likewise a fresh Parcel of superfine Silk
Worm Gut, no better ever seen in England, as fine as a
Hair, and as strong as Six, the only Thing for Trout, Carp,
and Salmon; the best Sort of Multiplying Brass Winches,
both stop and plain; Woved Hair and Silk Lines, and all
other Sorts of Lines for Angling; various Sorts of Reels
and Cases; and all Sorts of Pocket Books for Tackle,
Menow Kettles, and Nets to preserve Live Bait; Fishing
Paniers and Bags; Variety of Gentle-Boxes and Worm-
Bags; Landing-Nets and Hooks; Fishing-Stools; Wicker
and Leather Bottles; and many ther Curiosities, in the way
of Angling. All Sorts of Trunks to shoot Darts and Pellets.

Glossary

Antenna float
A float which has a long thin antenna projecting above the main buoyant portion; this cuts through the ripple in windy conditions — keeping the bait from 'jigging' with the ripples and thus making a more stable bite indicator.

Arlesy bomb
A pear-shaped leger lead with a swivel at the pointed end. The line passes through the swivel eye, and is carried down to the bottom (see leger).

Artery forceps
Forceps that look like scissors with tweezer ends instead of sharp points and which can be locked when a hold has been secured. By far the best and most humane way to extract hooks or flies.

Breaking strain
The manufacturer's estimate of the strength of his line, measured when dry. This usually is lower when the line is wet or knotted.

Cast
The action of throwing bait or flies onto the water using a rod and line. Also the name given to the length of nylon (usually tapered) which attaches the fly to the fly line.

Centre-pin reel
A drum reel — with the drum rotating freely on the same axis as the axis of the rod. The handle is usually fixed directly to the drum.

Devon minnow
A torpedo-shaped spinning bait painted to resemble a small fish. Vanes just behind the head cause it to spin when drawn through the water. It has a single treble hook at the rear end.

Disgorger
Instrument designed to remove hooks from fishes mouths (see also artery forceps).

Dry fly
An artificial fly dressed with suitable materials and in such a way that it will sit on the surface of the water.

Dun
A fly (that starts its life in the water as a nymph) just after it hatches out and before its wings are dry and ready for flight.

Fixed-spool reel
A reel that has its spool set at right angles to the axis of the rod. The spool remains stationary and the line is wound-on by a bale arm that rotates round the spool. The spool is fitted with a slipping clutch to enable a fish to take more line.

Float
A float is designed to indicate a bite. It is usually set so that it carries the bait above the bottom, though it can be set so that the bait lies on the bottom of the water. It is also used to carry bait along in the current, thus searching the swim. Floats may be designed to carry a lot of weight and therefore be cast a long way. They may be designed with the necessary weight already in them, so that they 'cock' or float vertically upon entering the water. These are known as self-cocking floats and require little or no weight to sink the bait. They are usually made to be fixed to the line — but can also be used without fixing so that they slide. This enables the bait to be fished at a depth greater than the length of the rod.

Floatant
A preparation, generally silicone based, to make flies and fly lines buoyant.

Fly line
A heavy line, generally made of plastic material on a braided core, usually 30—35 yards (27—32 m) long and may be tapered to enable it to be put down lightly on the water.

Fly reel
A centre-pin type of reel with the drum usually enclosed in a cage and fitted with a permanent check.

Gentles
A common name given to the maggots (or larvae) of the bluebottle.

Ground bait
A bait, usually similar to the hook bait, but thrown into the water in the area being fished — to attract fish to the swim or to keep them there.

Hackle
A feather tied across a hook and then wound round so that the fibres stick out to imitate the legs of a fly. Cock hackles, which are spikey, are used for dry flies because they stick out stiffly and help the fly to float. Hen hackles, which are soft, are used for wet flies as they aid

penetration into the surface of the water and 'work' beneath the surface in a life-like manner.

Lask
A strip of fish used as bait when sea-fishing. It is also called a last.

Leger
The name given to the method of fishing where the bait is held on the bottom by a lead having a swivel attached to it (or a hole in it) through which the line runs. A split shot is pinched onto the line, or a small strip of rubber knotted in, to form a stop and prevent the lead from sliding down to foul the hook and bait. When the fish bites, the line is drawn through the swivel eye this being signalled by an indicator on the rod or the line near the reel.

Multiplying reel
These reels come in many sizes, the smallest being used for freshwater spinning, then sea beach casting and the largest, for big game fishing. They are geared to retrieve quickly, and have spools that can be made free-running for distance casting. They also frequently have a drag to aid playing a fish and a moving guide to wind the line on evenly.

Nymph
The larval stage of an insect after it has hatched from its egg and is living and feeding under the water. When it comes to maturity, it rises to the surface or climbs onto weeds or pebbles, bursts out of its nymphal skin, spreads its wings to dry, and then takes off to mate.

Otter
A large floating object (a piece of cork or hollow plastic about saucer size, or length of wood) that can be attached to a line so that the line runs freely along or through it. This enables the otter to be floated beyond a trapped bait, where, by lifting the rod tip, a pull may be exerted in the opposite direction to free the bait.

Peeler
A common crab which is about to replace its shell. They make excellent bait for sea fish when the shell has been pulled off.

Plug
A wooden or plastic imitation fish, shaped or made with a vane so that it dives, darts or wobbles when retrieved. They may be made to float or to sink slowly.

Priest
The name given to a small truncheon, usually made of metal or weighted. Used to kill fish outright with a smart blow.

Pumping
The action used to raise a heavy fish in the water. The rod tip is lowered as line is wound onto the reel, and then the tip raised when one stops winding; the action is repeated until the fish is brought to the surface.

Spinner
A mature ephemerid fly — fully adult (immediately following the dun stage) and ready to mate.

Spinning
The casting and retrieving of a natural or artificial bait that is so shaped, or fitted, with vanes or fins, that it wobbles or spins in the water in a life-like way.

Split-shot
Lead shot of varying sizes, which have splits in them to allow the line to be placed in the split — and the shot then pinched to hold it in position on the line.

Spoon
A spoon-shaped spinning bait.

Strike
The short sharp lift of the rod tip which sets the hook point in the fish when a bite is indicated.

Swim
The area of water in which an angler is fishing.

Swivel
Two small metal eyes, connected to a barrel mounting, so that each eye can rotate independently. When used to connect two lengths of line, it prevents the possibility of kinking.

Trace
The name given to the length of stout nylon or wire that connects the hook or spinning bait to the line. Used for example when angling for fish that have teeth.

Treble
A hook with three barbs.

Wet fly
A fly usually tied with a soft swept-back hackle, swept-back wings of feather or hair, and frequently a body made of heavy materials so that it can be fished below the surface.